Interferences and Events

Interferences and Events: On Epistemic Shifts in Physics through Computer Simulations

edited by Anne Dippel and Martin Warnke

μ meson press

mecs

MEDIA CULTURES OF
COMPUTER SIMULATION

This publication is funded by MECS Institute for Advanced Study on
Media Cultures of Computer Simulation, Leuphana University Lüneburg
(German Research Foundation Project KFOR 1927).

Diese Publikation wurde unterstützt aus Mitteln der DFG-Kolleg-
Forschergruppe MECS Medienkulturen der Computersimulation,
Leuphana Universität Lüneburg (KFOR 1927).

Bibliographical Information of the German National Library
The German National Library lists this publication in the Deutsche
Nationalbibliografie (German National Bibliography); detailed
bibliographic information is available online at http://dnb.d-nb.de

Published by meson press, Lüneburg.
www.meson.press

Design concept: Torsten Köchlin, Silke Krieg
The print edition of this book is printed by Books on Demand,
Norderstedt, Germany

ISBN (Print): 978-3-95796-105-1
ISBN (PDF): 978-3-95796-106-8
ISBN (EPUB): 978-3-95796-107-5
DOI: 10.14619/022

The digital editions of this publication can be downloaded freely at:
www.meson.press

Contents

1

About Waves, Particles, Events, Computer Simulation, and Ethics in Quantum Physics

Anne Dippel and Martin Warnke

When Max Planck in 1874 asked one of his teachers, Philipp von Jolly, whether to choose physics as his discipline of academic study, he received the response that there was not much to be gained there. This trivia about Planck's life and the course of the history of science he himself influenced so much tells us: we never should be too sure that the gaining of knowledge is ever finished.

Despite von Jolly's opinion the beginning of the twentieth century brought about several surprises: with the appearance of Herman Minkowski's concept of space-time and Albert Einstein's annihilation of the ether that in the end led to the special and later the general theories of relativity, a first radical new branch of physics appeared. It was counterintuitive and yet scientifically highly successful at the same time. It revealed insights to the concepts of space and time and to problems of cosmology, to the very big of what we call "nature". But the high hopes that humankind would also soon know how to get hold of the world of very small were disappointed initially. The radiation of atoms and the behavior of subatomic particles that were discovered by that time seemed so strange that it was utterly unexplainable by contemporary physics of that period of time.

Then, as a second scientific surprise to the young century, that was about to shock humanity with an abundance of violent events in its further course, quantum mechanics entered the realm of physics.

Quantum mechanics, originally a theory developed by Planck to describe the black-body radiation problem, soon helped to explain atomic and subatomic phenomena. It had been evolving alongside experimental setups to a point of completion at the beginning of the 1930s. Thus, it provided new possibilities in describing the material world with a precision that was not achievable before. Nevertheless, it encoded into physics a rich collection of riddles and paradoxes, like the simultaneity of wave and particle perspectives, of "spooky actions at a distance," known as quantum entanglement, the decline of determinism, and the impossibility of simultaneously and exactly measuring well-known quantities like the location and velocity of a particle.

Physicists like Einstein were not satisfied with this situation of logical and conceptual inconsistencies—he once wrote "God doesn't play dice with the world"—and throughout the 20th century for beginners and lay people, as well as for experts such as the famous inventor of the diagrams for the interaction of subatomic particles named after him, Richard Feynman, the bewilderments of quantum theory are hard to accept on the one side and an invitation to esoteric speculation on the other. How can a thing be at the same time a wave and a particle? How can the state of one thing influence another instantaneously even though they are in two different, distant places? On the other hand, today, quantum mechanics proves to be the best tested theory in the history of physics. Therefore, experimentalists and theoreticians simply get used to the formalism that yields excellent predictions through the course of their education, and have to suppress the logical problems, since it works in the lab, and the lab has to work. The presuppositions about the behavior of nature turn into facts.

In the quantum world particles interact at a distance, and numerous experiments show, that they act as if under a spell of contagion cast by a witch. But science is not magic, and how can we understand nature to the fullest, when we're part of the system? The subatomic world seems to be formally describable, but from a logic perspective ungraspable for modern human beings. Even more when they are relying on logical devices such as the computer itself.

Physics students learn to deal with the ungraspable aspects of their discipline; many succumb at one point or another to the slogan "Shut up and calculate!" to cope pragmatically with the open problems of quantum mechanics, and even more so as their military and industrial applications require ever more young people being trained in it. Others try to overcome the theoretical problems by building experiments. This seems to suggest that pondering the philosophical implications and logical problems of quantum mechanics might be superfluous, since the math works and the experiments are producing results. The common attitude towards a mathematical apparatus that works so well reminds us of Martin Heidegger's prejudice about the sciences as disciplines that seem not be able to "think", because they "do", we might add.

Since the beginnings of quantum theory, thought experiments especially served as tools to work out the contradictions and peculiarities between a reasonable Newtonian world in which humans would live, and a theory of microscopic cabinet of wonder where nature shows its magic side. Of these experiments the one about the double slit is the most famous, the simplest and the one in which experimentation, theory, and computer simulations still meet with vivid intensity. It observes how particles behave if shot onto a twofold opening that allows for alternatives in their trajectory. Surprisingly enough, single particles produce interference patterns that are known, since then, to be phenomena of waves alone.

This experiment is usually attributed to the fundamental idea that individual elementary particles behave like waves, because the interference patterns on a screen far from the double slit only emerge if we do not know which of the slits they passed through, one by one. Since the introduction of the de Broglie wavelength and Schrödinger's matter wave equation, there is even the strong suggestion that seemingly indivisible particles pass through both slits at the same time.

The logical difficulty arises when an interpretation of the double-slit experiment tries to theorize individual particles that behave on their way through the experiment as if they were smeared out in space, although they are detected at distinctive places in the end. The concept of a matterwave and its inherent idea of self-interference of particles is hard to reconcile with measurements that in the end take place event by event. The notion of the event itself does not appear in traditional quantum theory, and at the end and the beginning of the experiment, in its Newtonian moment, matter shows itself as solid, not wavy, while in-between, the jiggly aspect of matter itself seems to appear; without that it can't be theorized.

Although the predictions of quantum theory show excellent experimental confirmation, quantum theory is not capable of describing the measurement process itself on the mathematical level. It is said that the wave function "collapses" at the event of the measurement, indicating the end of the quantum formalism. In the lab this normally takes place through the experimental observation of individual events, for example, the click of a detector. Quantum theory only allows for statistical predictions that can be tested by large numbers of measurements, never to statements about single events.

Now enter computer simulations!

With the development of event-based computer simulations new opportunities arise to describe the behavior of singular molecules as observed in quantum optical experiments of the double slit type. At the Institute for Advanced Study on the Media Cultures of Computer Simulation (MECS) in Lüneburg, Germany, we held a conference on the 20th and 21st of January 2016 to explore the contradictory phenomena of interferences and events from a logical perspective, as well as the dichotomy of the wave and particle images that quantum physics demands we deal with. We invited distinguished scientists and scholars from the fields of computational, theoretical, and experimental physics, and of the history and philosophy of science, in order to explore the potential of concepts and technologies emerging out of computer simulations to tackle unsolved problems at the theoretical heart of contemporary quantum mechanics. Can simulations not only provide descriptions and predictions for physics behavior, but also produce theories in their own right, which could compete with traditional theoretical concepts such as a differential equation-based theory of quantum mechanics?

In the interdisciplinary audience there were physicists, computer scientists, philosophers, game theorists, and scholars of literature, who would critically examine the presentations and contribute to the intense discussions that brought fresh perspectives on the epistemological role of computer simulations in physics and science in general, but also showed the robustness of contemporary quantum mechanical experimentation and theory.

By metaphorically using a quantum physics notation in the title of the conference, the <bras| and the |kets> of Paul Dirac, we illustrated our attempt to find out how much interference could be found in its opposing notion of events— and vice versa— by projecting them onto one another as: <interferences|events>, pronounced as "bra interferences ket events." In quantum mechanics such a term computes to what extent the state on the right, the |ket>, could be projected onto the state on the left, the <bra|. Arianna Borrelli wrote about this in her paper in this book. If there is a nonzero result for this quantum mechanical term—to use the slang of the discipline—then we would know more about the relationship between

those contradictory concepts and could then calculate the probability that one turned into the other.

Indeed, we found much more than just the void! This book documents the enlightening presentations and intense discussions we had during those two days. The table of contents follows the conference proceedings by thoroughly picturing the concurrent streams of thought that the subject ignites in people's minds. All the material and arguments are comprehensible to a wider audience and provide explanations that do not need a scientific education as a prerequisite. Formulas only appear as subjects of methodological investigation, and the arguments are made plausible without using the language of math.

Our first speakers, Kristel Michielsen and Hans De Raedt, both theoretical and computational physicists at the Jülich Research Centre talked about their approach to theory building and description of the aforementioned double-slit thought experiment—also actually performed in a lab later on— through the use of event-based computer simulations. Differently from the traditional approach of quantum mechanics, they model the whole process using events. A messenger is emitted by a source and processed by the experimental apparatus in a way that can be described by simple rules. At the end a sequence of individual events triggers a detection device that stands in for the measuring detectors in a laboratory. Instead of using the matrix- or differential equation-based mathematics developed by Werner Heisenberg, Erwin Schrödinger, Dirac and others that does not explain the behavior of single events but of collectives alone, a computer piles up results of discrete processes modeled by algorithms that then look similar to, if not indistinguishable from, laboratory data. In Michielsen and De Raedt's approach, everything is deterministic and there are no logical oddities in the whole process, unlike with the formalism of quantum physics that is normally applied without exception throughout the discipline. At the same time the results of the experimental quantum mechanical setups are perfectly reproduced. The tradition of logical reasoning based on computer simulations is put to an extreme perfection, ruling out all "spookiness" of quantum mechanics through media technology.

This marks the fascinating aspect of an event-based simulation attempt like the one described here: it only considers undoubtable properties of particles like their mass or spin, makes reasonable assumptions about experimental devices and does not rely on the so-called first principles used everywhere else, like the uncertainty principle or quantum states that can exist in superpositions as solutions to the Schrödinger equation in quantum theory. These principles are known as such because they are claimed to be the all-encompassing laws of a field that always hold true and from which all phenomena can be deduced. First principles have a similar grounding role as axioms in mathematics, but still have to stand an experimental test. The event-by-event approach is unparalleled in the hundred years of quantum research up to now, and only became possible because of the computing solutions available since the last three decades. This also means that physicists do not know through experience how far they can trust this method in cases where they do not have data from the lab. The only strategy to confirm the approach is to play a Turing's imitation game on the microscopic level, to judge just by the data what is a simulation and what is a lab process. If one cannot tell them apart, one may have to concede some credibility to this novel approach and place it as a computational solution alongside the existing mathematical approaches to describe the phenomena traditionally called "quantum."

At stake is the epistemological question of what relation exists between any formalism, be it traditional mathematics or novel computer simulations, and "nature" itself. Or, how cultural are the physical approaches to defining nature? Do mathematical theories of any kind say anything about nature itself or are they conceptual metaphors we learned to "live by" (Lakoff and Johnson [1980] 2003)?

The discussion after the presentation raised questions on the inclusion of the measurement event into quantum mechanics that in its current condition cannot deal with events at all, e. g. could not include the measurement operation itself. Subsequently was a debate about the collapse of the wave function, indicating the very border of the quantum formalism. Is there a "classical" world where the event of a measurement takes place and a separate "quantum" world where we have interferences from individual particles? The views on that differed across the audience.

Lukas Mairhofer, currently based in the Lukas Arndt-Group at Vienna Center for Quantum Science and Technology of Vienna University, gave the next presentation, on observing the unobservable and the quantum interference of complex macromolecules. Not only does Mairhofer reflect his work as a philosopher, he also does so as a passionate experimentalist. He provides a reflected glimpse into the contemporary practices of quantum mechanics, using multiple-slit experiments in the lab, where theoretical perspectives guide experimental work at any time. In a quantum mechanical experiment the logical problems of quantum theory turn into those of "practical" labor: the physicists fill one side of a complex technical apparatus with a grainy material consisting of visible particles—and nevertheless are forced to assume that it behaves like a matter wave on the way through the experimental system, passing optical grids where every molecule interferes with itself. At the end the detector counts discrete clicks that sum up to an interference patterns of a wave phenomenon. Contrary to the event-by-event simulative approach of the speakers before is the use of traditional quantum mechanics as the grounding theory. But Mairhofer and the whole Vienna Quantum Optics group go well beyond what could be done theoretically nowadays: they measure in regions where theoretical calculation is still impossible. Experimental verification is at the very core of the epistemic process in physics, and so the quantum optical setups in Vienna provide crucial indications of what could be known in the science of physics.

In the discussion experimental details were explored and philosophical questions were debated, such as the translation of subatomic behavior into the "classical world": What would it mean to be delocalized as a human being, as during the quantum mysteries of matter spread out in space as a matter wave? Mairhofer ends his talk with a prospect: What would it mean if living matter, like viruses, was subject to self-interference in the double-slit experiment?

Since in a contemporary quantum optical laboratory an experimental setup without computers is impossible, theoretical questions about media arose: What is the contribution of contemporary simulations to quantum optical experiments? Is what Mairhofer does in his experiments in itself already a simulation? What relationship exists between experiment and computer simulation in general? Is experimentation more of a simulation than science believed it to be up to now?

The next speaker, Mira Maiwöger, works as an experimental physicist in the Atomchip group of Jörg Schmiedmayer at the Atominstitut in Vienna. In her experiments the concept of matter waves also takes an important role. Her experiment investigates so-called Bose–Einstein condensates (BECs), which come into being, according to quantum theory, when big lumps of matter, say a spoonful, assemble in one big quantum state. This happens when matter is cooled down to extremely low temperatures. The speciality of her experiment is to prepare matter under extreme conditions, creating states that are also interesting theoretically, and then drawing conclusions for other materials that cannot be forced into these modes of existence in the same way. Experimentation becomes a kind of simulation of one system by another.

Maiwöger explains how one simulates magnetic material by observing BECs in rubidium. This analog simulation does not use algorithms to mimic a system of interest, but exploits the concept of similitude, of vicarious relationships.

Since all that work is embedded into a theoretical context, one which claims that particular systems are similar in a conceptual respect, the experiments not only probe physical systems but also physical theory, all this by analog simulation. To take one example, there is the theoretical concept of the superposition of states, say a right turning and a left turning one, essential to quantum mechanics and yet absolutely impossible from the perspective of classical physics, where something cannot turn right and left at the same time. To directly deal with these phenomena is like bringing the disturbing aspects of quantum physics into a material, directly observable being, all without taking resort to computers.

In the vivid discussion on the work currently done at the Viennese Atomin-stitut, philosophical aspects of the onto-epistemology of the quantum world explored by Karen Barad were elucidated. The framework of "agential realism" (Barad 2007) delivers a fruitful approach to also understanding why event-based simulations could equally explain the seemingly con-tradictory subatomic world of the from a classical perspective. Maiwöger showed what "non-natural nature," or natureculture (Law 2010), itself could actually be if put under the conditions of experimental physics: obviously it is not the privilege of computer simulations to create artificial realities, but as has been stated throughout the last decade by researchers from different fields in the realm of science and technology studies, physics itself produces realities that are neither pure nature, nor culture.

One goal of the conference was to clarify the relationship between event-based computer simulations and physical theory. As trained theoretical physicist and expert in building, as well as simulating robots with computers, Frank Pasemann from Osnabrück University seemed to be the right person to ponder about a possible need for new kinds of theory with the presence of computer simulations in theoretical physics. He showed some criteria of sound physical theories to discuss whether computer simulations themselves could be thought of as theories on their own, but remains undecided on the matter and expects further evidence in the future. Nevertheless, he states the obvious influences of computer simulations on theory building in physics, the full consequences of which are not yet known.

In the discussion afterwards comparisons with other disciplines such as biology helped to question whether researchers are used to describing phenomena without having something that could be called a theory altogether, and how theoretical trends and habits emerge and vanish over time.

The next speaker, Arianna Borrelli, a historian of physics and a trained physicist herself, working at the MECS as well as at the Technical University of Berlin, gave us impressions from the history of quantum physics about how contemporary computer simulations might be regarded as a type of theory. She did that by pointing us to the creative functions of notation; how the notions of a theoretical framework are actually written down normally slips our attention. She described the eminent role that a specific form of the expression of abstract concepts plays in the development of a physical theory, for example, notational systems as media that influence our thinking. Interestingly enough even the concrete forms of such expressions seem to have haptical and sensual sides to them and can be regarded as "embodied theories." She showed this by recalling that the algebraic terms for the atomic spectra of radiation entered science unexpectedly by the way of perspective drawings, and that Dirac and others bent mathematical concepts far beyond the areas justified by mathematical proof in order to invent physically "interesting" notations, done so by using infinite or even continuous matrices.

From that perspective, computer simulations could be seen as another way of embodying theoretical concepts into a different material form, equally as valid as mathematical notations.

In the following discussion the close resemblance between creative notational methodologies and computer simulations became much clearer. The stage was now set for an even broader perspective on the vicarious relationships between different areas of scientific research. Having started <interferences|events> with the question about in which way event-based computer simulations could be producing physical theories in their own right, the conference now realized that this was not the only structure for exploiting the similitude between different parts of physical science. Not only computer simulations stand in for physical systems: One physical system mimics another, notational formalisms are precursors to mathematics, and, as we will see, one theory can stand in for another.

Leuphana-based media theorist Wolfgang Hagen gave a historiographical account of how Heinrich Hertz was simulating electromagnetism using elasticity theory. He explored the transitions between those fields and showed a historical example of a very conscious and skeptical use of parallelisms between fields of knowledge. The similitude and the analogy didn't need to be perfect in every aspect; the incompleteness of any formalism describing nature was much clearer in Hertz's times than it is nowadays, when theory becomes so successful that it seems to be without alternative.

Again Barad's concept of agential realism served as a discursive spring-board to discussing the ethics of "not knowing" and the impact of media on scientific interventions and representations, as well as the relationship between nature and culture. Finally, the discussion turned again to the central topic pursued at MECS, which is the influence of computer simulations on scientific thinking, of how to think of them as "inneres Scheinbild" (mental images) in the way Hertz used the term.

The last presentation of the conference was an intervention by historian of science and biologist Hans-Jörg Rheinberger, who emphasized the special epistemological status and role of experimental systems. He asked stimulating questions, such as: Would it be possible for computer simulations to produce new knowledge about nature as explorative experiments do? What is the relation between computer simulations and thought experiments? And if, like Niels Bohr put it, theory is on what we know about nature and not about nature itself, what then are computer simulations? Finally, could quantum theory be seen as an experimental way of knowing?

The general discussion led us back to the work of Michielsen and De Raedt, reiterating the questions about ontology and the realm of theoretical description overall.

This last roundtable served to sum up the thoughts of the participants. Computer simulations as creators of a new type of theory could open up the discovery of new phenomena unseen by traditional theories and should be included by the experimentalists in their research. A glimpse into the history of science and of disciplines other than physics, such as biology, shows that different relations between theory and experimentation or discovery in general evolve during the course of the history of an academic discipline. A great deal of complexity and richness is lost if the only guide to discovery is what traditional theory is pointing us to and what published scientific papers reveal from the research process. Also inspired by biology the question arose of what life is if it gets into the computer? How does mathematics relate to the state of being alive?

The discussion touched on the plurality of today's approaches in physics and how by mutual inspiration different fields such as computational and quantum physics could end up finding new insights by testing computational-based hypotheses on the one hand and analyzing experimental data thrown away before—because they were thought of as "useless", that is, not complying to traditional theories—on the other.

The crucial loop between theory and experiment, the quest for reproducibility, the whole epistemological apparatus of a positive, exact science, now seemingly enter into a crisis because of experiments that are very difficult or even impossible to reproduce.

At the end of the conference the importance of ethics with regard to the impact of computer simulations in science brought together all the disciplines assembled here, asking for an interdisciplinary approach that would lead to the establishment of ethics of design in simulation—thoughts that are related to discussions already led by Bertolt Brecht and Hans Reichenbach in the early era of quantum mechanics.

The times when it was enough to "shut up and calculate" are over. While computer-simulations contributed to the climate of "philosophobia" in physics in the first place, new modes of doing simulations are opening long-time black-boxed topics of how this discipline conceptualizes nature and the relation of the observer to what can be observed. Go ahead and start to think anew by reading yourself what the participants of <interferences|events> had to say.

References

Barad, Karen. 2007. *Meeting the Universe Halfway: Quantum Physics and the Entanglement of Matter and Meaning*. Durham, NC: Duke University Press.

Lakoff, George, and Mark Johnson. (1980) 2003. *Metaphors We Live By*. Chicago: University of Chicago Press.

Law, John. 2010. "Enacting Naturecultures. A Note from STS," *On-Line Papers of the Centre for Science Studies, Lancaster University*, accessed April 2017, http://www.lancaster.ac.uk/fass/resources/sociology-onlne-papers/papers/law-enacting-naturecultures.pdf.

2

Discrete-Event Simulation of Quantum Physics Experiments

Kristel Michielsen and Hans De Raedt

In one of his review articles Anton Zeilinger mentioned in 1999 that in former times one could only rely on *Gedanken* (thought) experiments to discuss the foundations of quantum physics, but that because of the tremendous experimental progress in recent years it became possible to base this discussion on actually performed experiments (Zeilinger 1999). Apart from these two options there is a third option to help contribute to this debate, namely performing computer simulations emulating thought and laboratory experiments. For the foundations of quantum physics, this requires a change of paradigm. In traditional, theoretical modeling the behavior of physical systems is described in terms of mathematical models. Usually differential equations, probability theory and so on are used to describe the system and its behavior. In this paper we replace this traditional modeling with a discrete-event simulation in which we model physical phenomena as chronological sequences of events. Although in the discrete-event approach we describe the behavior of systems in terms of simple rules, collectively these systems may exhibit complex behavior. Well-known examples of this approach are the Lattice Boltzmann model, used to simulate the flow of complex fluids, and the cellular automata from Stephen Wolfram (Wolfram 2002).

The community "Collective Evolution," which promotes thinking outside of the box, published on their website their top three mind-boggling quantum experiments (Walia 2015). The first experiment on their list is the double-slit experiment with electrons, photons, atoms, molecules, etc., in which the interference pattern is built up event by event. Quantum theory explains this experiment by introducing the concept of particle–wave duality: the property of particles behaving as waves and waves behaving as waves and particles. The second experiment on their list is the delayed choice/quantum eraser experiment. It is often said that this experiment illustrates how what happens in the present can change what happened in the past. The third experiment is an experiment for measuring quantum entanglement, such as the Einstein–Podolsky–Rosen–Bohm experiment for example. In such an experiment it appears that one particle of an entangled pair "knows" what measurement has been performed on the other one and what the outcome of that measurement is, even though there is no known means of information exchange between the particles. Explanations of the observations are sometimes formulated in terms of Einstein's "spooky action at a distance."

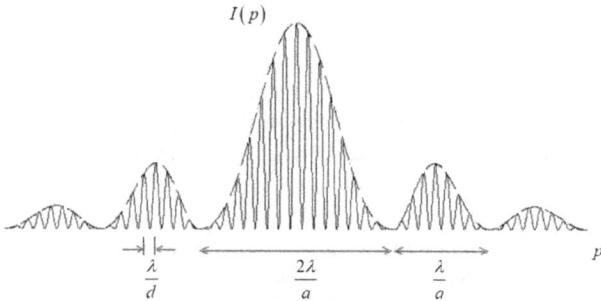

[Fig. 1] Fraunhofer interference pattern $I(p)$ for a source emitting monochromatic light with wavelength λ and angle of incidence θ_0 thereby illuminating a plate with two line-shaped slits with width a and center-to-center distance d. Here $p = \sin\theta - \sin\theta_0$ where θ denotes the angle of refraction. The solid line comes from the two-slit interference and the dashed line comes from the single-slit diffraction (see footnote 2).

The single-particle double-slit experiment is one of the most fundamental experiments in quantum physics and thus our focus for this paper. The structure of the paper is as follows. In the first section we briefly recall how to calculate the interference pattern for a two-slit experiment with classical light. We discuss the event-by-event buildup of the interference pattern in two-slit experiments with massive objects (electrons, neutrons) in the second section. As we review in section three, usually quantum theory is used to describe these experiments in terms of single particles, single wave packets or an ensemble interpretation of quantum mechanics. Except for the latter interpretation which is silent on the issue of events, all other descriptions suffer from some logical inconsistencies. In the fourth section we use a different approach to explain the event-by-event buildup of the interference pattern, namely the discrete-event simulation approach. The last section summarizes our conclusions.

Two-Slit Experiment with Light

The first two-slit experiment with light was performed by Thomas Young in 1801. In the basic form of this experiment a monochromatic point source is emitting light that falls on a plate with two pinholes that are close together and equidistant from the source. The light passing through the pinholes is observed on a screen placed far behind the plate. The two pinholes act as secondary point sources which emit monochromatic light beams that are in phase. Due to the wave character of the light, light waves passing through the pinholes interfere, thereby producing a pattern of bright and dark bands on the screen, the so-called interference pattern.

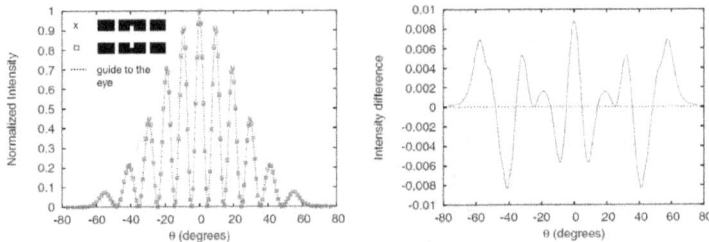

[Fig. 2] Left: Simulated interference pattern for two different two-slit configurations. The metal plate with refractive index $n = 2.29 + 2.61i$ and height 4λ has two slits of width λ separated by a center-to-center distance of 6λ. In the middle between the two slits is an indent of width λ and height 2λ. In one of the two-slit configurations the indent is located at the bottom of the plate (x marks) and in the other configuration at the top of the plate (square marks). The plate is illuminated by light with a wavelength $\lambda = 500\,\text{nm}$. Right: Difference between the two interference patterns.

From the theory of optics (Born and Wolf 1964) it follows, after performing some relatively simple mathematical calculations using pen and paper, that the interference pattern depends on the wavelength λ and the angle of incidence θ_0 of the monochromatic light emitted by the two point sources, and on the distance d between the two sources.[1] In most two-slit

---

1   In detail: the intensity pattern is given by $I(p) = \cos^2(kdp/2)$ with $p = \sin\theta - \sin\theta_0$ where θ denotes the angle of refraction and $k = 2\pi/\lambda$.

experiments that are carried out in the laboratory the slits cannot be described as pinholes acting as point sources.

A more accurate representation of the slit is a line-shaped slit. The Fraunhofer diffraction pattern observed on a screen placed at a large distance from an illuminated plate that contains two line slits with width a and center-to-center distance d is shown in Fig. 1.[2] But, in laboratory experiments the interference patterns differ from this "ideal" two-slit interference pattern. The cause of these differences is that the assumptions under which the Fraunhofer formula has been derived do not apply: apart from a width slits also have a height and depth and/or the distance between the source and detection screen and/or the source and the plate with the slits might be too small, and/or the slit width is not small enough compared to the source–plate and plate–detector screen distances. Taking into account the experimental details in a derivation of the interference pattern requires more than pen and paper: one has to rely on computer simulations. An example demonstrating that slits cannot simply be replaced by secondary sources and that details in the experimental setup matter for the resulting interference pattern is shown in Fig. 2. It depicts the simulation results for the interference patterns of two different two-slit configurations with an indent between the two slits (De Raedt, Michielsen, and Hess 2012). The results have been obtained by solving the time-dependent Maxwell equation on JUQUEEN (Stephan and Docter 2015), one of the largest supercomputers in Europe. The results show an intensity difference of 0.8%, and this is for an "ideal case simulation." Even small details in the setup of the devices like indents or other constructive elements obviously matter! A calculation in which the slits were replaced by secondary sources would not show this difference.

Two-Slit Interference with Objects: Experiments

These experiments belong to the class of so-called quantum experiments. As mentioned in the introduction, in former times one had to rely on *Gedanken* experiments to study questions related to the foundations of quantum mechanics. In 1964 Richard Feynman formulated a thought experiment for studying the two-slit interference experiment with electrons (Feynman, Leighton, and Sands 1965). The experiment consists of

2   The diffraction pattern of one line source with width a reads $I(p) = [(\sin(^{\kappa a p}/_2))/(^{\kappa a p}/_2)]^2$ (dashed line in Fig. 1). The Fraunhofer formula for the interference pattern observed on a screen placed at a large distance from the illuminated plate that contains two line slits with width a and center-to-center distance d reads $I(p) = \cos^2(^{\kappa d p}/_2)$ $[(\sin(^{\kappa a p}/_2))/(^{\kappa a p}/_2)]^2$ (solid line in Fig. 1).

an electron gun emitting individual electrons in the direction of a thin metal plate with two slits in it, behind which is placed a movable detector. According to Feynman: (1) one could hear from the detector sharp identical "clicks," which are distributed erratically; (2) the probability $P_1(x)$ or $P_2(x)$ of arrival, through one slit with the other slit closed, at position x is a symmetric curve with its maximum located at the center of the open slit; and (3) the probability $P_{12}(x)$ of arrival through both slits looks like the intensity of water waves propagated through two holes, thereby forming a so-called interference pattern, and looks completely different from the curve $P_1(x) + P_2(x)$ that would be obtained by repeating the experiment with bullets. These observations led Feynman to the conclusions that: (1) electrons arrive at the detector in identical "lumps," like particles; (2) the probability of arrival of these lumps is distributed like the distribution of intensity of a wave propagated through both holes; and (3) it is in this sense that an electron behaves "sometimes like a particle and sometimes like a wave,"—puzzling behavior for which the concept of particle–wave duality has been introduced. Feynman's general conclusion about the single-electron two-slit experiment was: "The observation that the interference pattern is built up event-by-event is impossible, absolutely impossible to explain in any classical way and has in it the heart of quantum mechanics. In reality it is the only mystery."

Although Feynman wrote "you should not try to set up this experiment" because "the apparatus would have to be made on an impossibly small scale to show the effects we are interested in," advances in (nano) technology made possible various laboratory implementations of his fundamental thought experiment. In what follows we discuss a selection of these experiments.

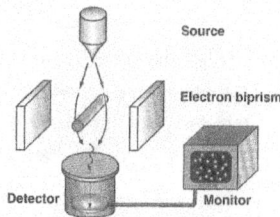

[Fig. 3] Scheme of the setup of the single-electron two-slit experiment (Tonomura 1998).

The first real single-electron interference experiments that were conducted were electron biprism experiments in which single electrons pass to the left or the right of a conducting wire (there are no real slits in this type of experiment) (see Merli, Missiroli, and Pozzi 1976; Tonomura et al. 1989). A scheme of the setup of the experiment of Tonomura and coworkers is shown in Fig. 3. The setup consists of an electron source, a biprism consisting of a wire and two plates, a detector, and a monitor. In this experiment at any time only one electron travels from the source to the detector. Each electron passes either to the left or the right of the wire before being detected by the detector, which results in a spot on the monitor. After many (about 50,000) electrons have been recorded an interference pattern emerges. Hence, although there is no interaction between the electrons they build up an interference pattern one by one.

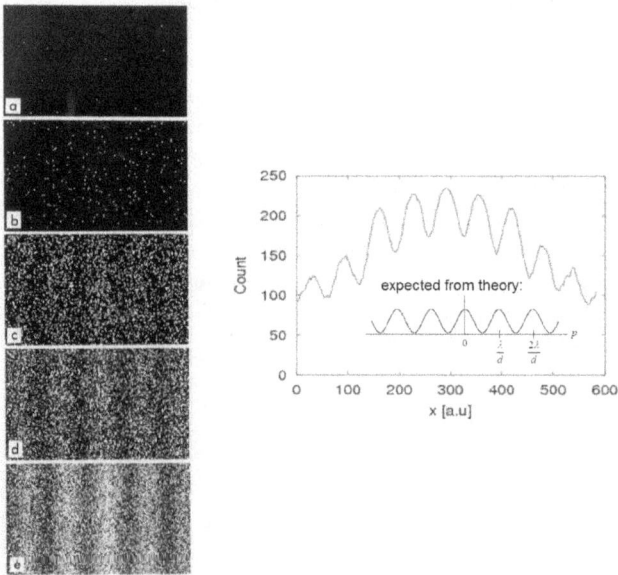

[Fig. 4] Left: Recordings of a single-electron double-slit experiment performed by Tonomura and coworkers showing the buildup of an interference pattern with an increasing number of detected electrons. Numbers of electrons are 11 (a), 200 (b), 6,000 (c), 40,000 (d), 140,000 (e) (Tonomura et al. 1989). Right: Final interference pattern. The inset shows the interference pattern expected from theory.

The buildup of the interference pattern is depicted in the left panel of Fig. 4. If the number of detected electrons is small, then the single spots on the monitor screen seem to be positioned randomly; after a larger number of electrons have been detected stripes are formed. From these observations one could conclude that electrons are detected one by one as particles. The right panel of Fig. 4 shows the intensity pattern obtained from the stripe pattern at the end of the experiment. The intensity pattern differs from what would be expected from theory for the ideal experiment but it does show interference. This interference pattern is often said to be formed when electron waves pass both sides of the wire at the same time. Hence, it is concluded that electrons in this experiment show both particle and wave character.

Rather recently, another realization of Feynman's thought experiment has been performed making use of a plate with two slits instead of an electron biprism (Bach et al. 2013). In this experiment a movable mask is placed behind the double-slit structure to open/close the slits. Unfortunately, the mask is positioned behind the slits and not in front of them, so all the electrons encounter the double-slit structure and are filtered afterwards by the mask. One could therefore argue that as of 2017 Feynman's thought experiment has still not been performed.

Interference experiments can also be performed with "objects" other than electrons. One example is the single-photon interference experiment of Jacques and coworkers (Jacques et al. 2005). This experiment is similar in spirit to that of Tonomura and coworkers except that photons are used instead of electrons. The experimental setup consists of a single-photon source, a prism with a very shallow angle that splits the beam (a so-called Fresnel biprism), and a detector. After many single detection events an interference pattern is observed. Another example is the single-neutron two-slit experiment of Zeilinger and coworkers (Zeilinger et al. 1988; Gähler and Zeilinger 1991), which is also of the same type as Tonomura's experiment. The setup consists of a neutron source, a wire, and two glass plates. As in the other experiments, care is taken that only one "object," in this case a neutron, at a time is ever traveling through the setup so that there can be no interaction between the neutrons. Also in this experiment, after many neutrons have been detected one by one, an interference pattern is seen. In this experiment the dimensions of the double slit are measured with an optical microscope and are also obtained by fitting curves to the experimentally measured interference pattern. Both methods give different results for the dimensions of the double slit, showing that the reality of an actual lab is much more complicated than the world of the *Gedanken* experiment. It is quite common practice to first extract the double slit dimensions from the experimental data by fitting them to Fraunhofer-like diffraction formulas and then comparing the measured interference pattern to the one obtained by numerical simulation with the extracted double slit dimensions.

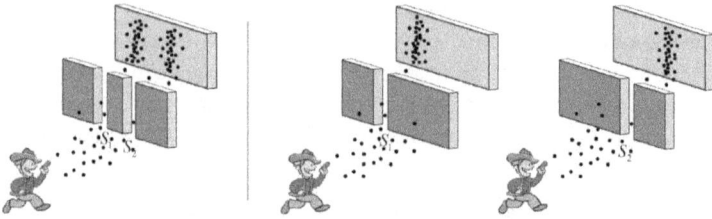

[Fig. 5] Left: Two-slit interference experiment with bullets. Right: Two one-slit experiments with bullets.

The original goal of the two-slit experiments was to demonstrate that not only waves but also "objects" (particles) can interfere. This original goal has shifted to obtaining interference with "objects" that are as large as possible, such as large organic molecules.

Two-Slit Interference with Entities: Description-Explanation

From now on we will call electrons, photons, neutrons, atoms and molecules "entities." It is important to stress that entities are indivisible units; in other words, they cannot split. In the two-slit interference experiments one click of the detector is associated with one entity arriving at the detector. Only after many single detection events does an interference pattern emerge. The interference patterns can be fitted by wave diffraction theory. The so-called dual particle-like and wave-like behavior of the entities can be explained in different ways. In what follows we discuss some of these explanations.

Entities are Particle Like

If the entities are particle like, then the two-slit experiment is well described by Feynman's interference experiment with bullets. Fig. 5 shows such an experiment in which we replaced Feynman's machine gun with a shooting cowboy. The cowboy shoots one bullet at a time towards a front wall that has one or two openings. The position of the cowboy with respect to the front wall is the same for each experimental setting. The positions of the openings in the front wall in the single-slit experiments correspond to their respective positions in the front wall in the double-slit experiment. In cases where the cowboy is shooting towards the wall with two openings labeled S_1 and S_2, the bullet passes through one slit or the other and arrives at a certain position on the rear wall that serves as a shield (a bullet is indivisible but one cannot observe through which slit it passes) or is stopped by the front wall. In cases where the cowboy is shooting towards one of the front walls with only one opening, labeled S_1 or S_2, the bullet passes through this single slit and arrives at a certain position on the rear wall or is stopped by the front wall. After the three experiments are finished one observes that the bullet hole pattern of the two-slit experiment is equal to the overlay, the sum of the bullet hole patterns of the two one-slit experiments. There is no interference. And if the bullets had been electrons, this is in contradiction to the observations made in the Tonomura experiment!

Any probabilistic theory, hence also quantum theory, describing these experiments postulates the existence of an underlying probabilistic process that determines the patterns with which the bullets will be observed. However, in these probabilistic descriptions the probabilities are conditional on the fact that a slit is open or closed—conditional probabilities with different conditions cannot be added (Ballentine 2003)[3]. In the case at hand, probability theory does not allow the addition of the probabilities of the single-slit shootings in any theoretical description of the process! Nevertheless, Feynman (and many others) did so because he simply forgot about the conditions.

Hence, although the naïve conclusion that the observed interference patterns in two-slit experiments with "entities" cannot be obtained with entities passing one by one through the double-slit device might at first sight seem correct, we will demonstrate in the section entitled "Two-slit

---

3   In the two-slit experiment with bullets one may get the impression that it is allowed to add conditional probabilities with different conditions, which are derived from the experimentally observed frequencies: $\sum_x P(x \mid S_1, S_2, Z) = 1$ is equal to $\sum_x P(x \mid \overline{S_1}, S_2, Z) + \sum_x P(x \mid S_1, \overline{S_2}, Z) = 0.5 + 0.5 = 1$. Here, x denotes a position on the detection screen, $S_j (\overline{S_j})$ corresponds to an open (closed) j-th slit ($j = 1,2$) and Z denotes all other identical conditions under which the three different experiments are carried out (e.g. the position of the shooting cowboy, the positions of the slits, the cowboy shoots half of the bullets in the direction of each slit, …). In general, one is not allowed to add conditional probabilities with different conditions, as can be seen from considering the following three experiments with variables (negations are represented by an overbar) R denoting that it rains, W representing that one gets wet from rain only, U denoting the fact that one has a very large umbrella that one uses not to get wet from rain, and Z are all other identical conditions in the different experiments: (1) it rains and one does not have a very large umbrella, (2) it does not rain and one has a very large umbrella, and (3) it rains and one has a very large umbrella. In this example $P(W \mid R, U, Z) = 0$ can definitely not be equal to $P(W \mid R, \overline{U}, Z) + P(W \mid \overline{R}, U, Z) = 1 + 0 = 1$.

interferences with entities: discrete-event simulations" that this is in fact not the case.

Entities are Wave Packets (Wave Like)

Under this assumption the picture is that a wave packet with a size larger than the center-to-center separation of the slits plus the slit width impinging on a double-slit device interferes with itself. According to quantum theory the time evolution of the wave packet is governed by the time-dependent Schrödinger equation $i\hbar\partial\psi(x, t)/\partial t = H\psi(x, t)$, where H denotes the Hamiltonian of the two-slit system, $\psi(x, t)$ represents the wave function of the complete system, and $\hbar$ is Planck's constant. Fig. 6 depicts a snapshot of a movie showing the time evolution of a Gaussian wave packet impinging on a double-slit device and thereby being partly reflected and partly transmitted. However, although the initial wave packet is split in two parts, at any time there is only one wave function, $\psi(x, t)$. What is actually shown in Fig. 6 is the intensity $|\psi(x, t)|^2$, which according to the Born rule gives the probability of finding the entity at position x. The "large" trans-mitted part of the wave packet emanating from the double slit reaches the detection screen. Thinking of the laboratory experiments, one expects the wave packet to produce one single spot on the screen because in exper-iments one does not observe the single interference of one entity.

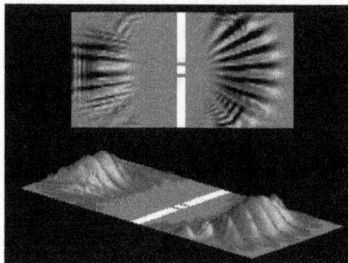

[Fig. 6] Intensity of a Gaussian wave packet of width $\sigma = 10\lambda$ reflected and transmitted by a wall with two slits in it (Michielsen and De Raedt 2012). The thickness of the wall is λ. The slits have a width $a = \lambda$ and a center-to-center distance $d = 4\lambda$. The initial wave packet moves from the left to the right.

Note that what should happen to the reflected part of the wave packet that is moving in the direction of the source is unclear. Heisenberg introduced in 1927 the reduction and Bohm in 1951 the collapse of a wave function to explain how a single entity represented as a wave packet can give rise to a single spot on a screen. However, this does not explain the event-by-event buildup of the interference pattern, i.e. the coordination between the detection events resulting from many "large" wave packets arriving at the detection screen. How should one explain this—by Einstein's spooky action at a distance? After almost 100 years, the collapse of the wave function remains elusive and does not provide a rational explanation of the observations in a two-slit experiment with single entities.

Ensemble Interpretation of the Interference Pattern

According to Einstein, "The attempt to conceive the quantum mechanical description as the complete description of individual systems leads to unnatural theoretical interpretations, which become immediately unnecessary if one accepts the interpretation that the description refers to ensembles of systems and not to individual systems" (Einstein 1949). In other words, one should not try to explain *individual* events using quantum theory.

Interpreting the wave packet (see e.g. Fig. 6) as one probability wave, representing the collection of all entities that is propagated through the double-slit device according to the rules of quantum theory, leads to an interference pattern that is similar to the final one observed in a laboratory experiment. However, this ensemble interpretation gives no clue about how to get from the final probability distribution to the detection events observed in the experiment. Events can simply not be "derived" from quantum theory (or from probability theory). Hence, the ensemble interpretation cannot explain the event-by-event buildup of the interference experiment.

Clearly we have here a dilemma. If, as Einstein said, we refrain from making statements about individual events, quantum theory is logically consistent. For atomic spectra quantum theory even gives a quantitative description. However, for the outcome of single-entity interference experiments or of experiments in which entanglement is involved quantum theory often only gives a qualitative description. This raises the question: how can it be that we have a very successful theory (quantum theory) that says nothing about the individual observations that make up the collective which the theory (quantum theory) describes very well?

As quantum theory cannot say anything about individual observations, another question that arises is whether it is possible to conceive ways of producing the kind of events that we observe in experiment directly, without referring to the concepts of quantum theory. The answer to this question is affirmative. For many of the so-called fundamental quantum physics experiments it is possible to construct a fairly universal computer simulation model that reproduces the results of all these experiments through discrete-event simulation, without solving wave equations and the like: for example see (De Raedt, De Raedt and Michielsen 2005; Michielsen, Jin and De Raedt 2011; De Raedt, Jin and Michielsen 2012; Michielsen and De Raedt 2014).

Two-Slit Interferences with Entities: Discrete-Event Simulations

Discrete-event simulation is a very general form of computer-based modeling. It provides a flexible approach to represent the behavior of complex systems in terms of a sequence of well-defined events; that is, operations performed by processors on entities of certain types. The entities themselves are passive, but they have attributes that affect the way they and their attributes are handled by the processors. Typically, many details about the entities are ignored. The events occur at discrete points in time. The system does not change between consecutive events. Discrete-event simulation is used in a wide range of health care, manufacturing, logistics, science, and engineering applications. We use discrete-event simulation to model various single-entity experiments relevant to the foundations of quantum physics.

In contrast to standard mathematical modeling, discrete-event simulation starts directly from experimental observations. In discrete-event modeling one searches for a logically consistent, cause-and-effect description of the definite results (the events) that constitute the experimental facts. Hence, one goes from events to probabilities and not vice versa. Therefore, the algorithm in a discrete-event simulation cannot refer to a probability distribution to produce the events. The resulting model may or may not fit into classical (Hamiltonian) mechanics. As in discrete-event modeling one starts from human perception, then goes to events, and finally arrives at a quantitative description, there is no need for an "objective" mathematical world picture. In our discrete-event simulation of single-entity experiments quantum theory emerges through inference from the events. We illustrate this with two examples related to two-slit interference with single photons.

Two-Slit Experiment with Two Beams (Two Sources)

From the theory of optics it follows that Young's double-slit experiment can be simplified to a two-beam experiment by replacing the two slits with two virtual sources. The two-beam experiment allows us to study interference in its most pure form because in contrast to the two-slit experiment the phenomenon of diffraction is absent. A time-resolved two-beam experiment has been performed in the laboratory (Garcia, Saveliev, and Sharonov 2002).

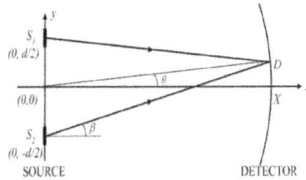

[Fig. 7] Schematic diagram of a two-beam experiment with light sources S_1 and S_2 of width a, separated by a center-to-center distance d. Both sources emit coherent, monochromatic light. The angles of emission β are uniformly distributed. The light is recorded by detectors D positioned on a semicircle with radius X and center $(0,0)$. The angular position of a detector is denoted by θ.

A schematic setup of the two-beam experiment with coherent, monochromatic light sources is shown in Fig. 7. In a single-photon version of the experiment the single-photon sources emit photons one by one. In the discrete-event model of this single-photon experiment entities are created one at a time by one of the sources (creation events) and are detected by one of the detectors forming the detection screen (detection events). We assume that all detectors are identical and cannot communicate with each other. We also assume that there is no direct communication between the entities (there is always only one entity between the source and the detector plane). Hence, the discrete-event model is *locally causal* by construction. If the entities build up an interference pattern one by one, then the interference pattern can only be due to the internal operation of the detectors, which has to be more complicated than just counting the incoming entities. We disregard the option that a similar interference pattern can be obtained by adding the detection events from a huge set of detectors that each only detected one entity. We do not consider this option, which is based on the statistical property of quantum theory, because there is no experimental evidence that replacing detectors after having detected an entity and then combining all these detection events indeed results in an interference pattern. The discrete-event simulation is based on observations made in laboratory experiments and not on hypothetical theoretical considerations.

Fig. 8 illustrates the general idea behind the discrete-event simulation approach. Simple rules define discrete-event processes that may lead to the behavior observed in experiments. The basic strategy in designing these rules is to carefully examine the experimental procedure and to devise rules such that they produce the same kind of input and output data as those recorded in the experiment. Evidently, mainly because of insufficient knowledge, the rules are not unique. Hence, the simplest rules one could think of can be used until a new experiment indicates otherwise. Obviously, the discrete-event simulation approach is concerned with what we can say about these experiments but not what "really" happens in nature.

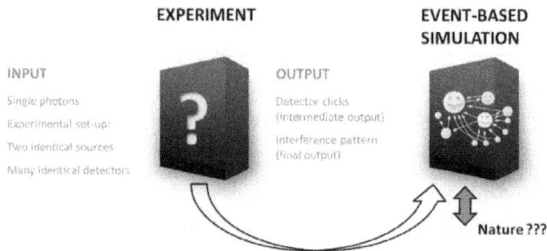

[Fig. 8] Schematic of the working principle of the discrete-event simulation approach. The first step consists of a detailed analysis of the experiment. Information about the input, such as characteristics of the source(s) and all other components in the experimental setup, and the output, such as the detector clicks (intermediate output) and the interference pattern or correlation (final output), including the data analysis procedure, is collected. It is assumed that it is not known how the input is transformed into the output. In a second step the "black box" that connects input and output in the experiment is replaced by a set of simple rules that transform this input into the same output. The frequently asked question about whether the rules describe what is going on in nature cannot be answered because the information necessary to answer this question is lacking.

The general picture in the discrete-event approach is that the entities are seen as messengers that carry certain messages, such as polarization, time, frequency, and so on, and run around in the experimental setup. The optical components in the experiment, in this case the two sources and the detectors, are seen as processors that interpret and manipulate the messages. It is important that the messengers do not communicate directly, only indirectly through the processors. This complies with the notion of local causality.

We now specify in a bit more detail the set of simple rules for simulating the two-beam, single-photon experiment. More detailed information can be found elsewhere (De Raedt and Michielsen 2012).

- Photons: The photon is regarded as a messenger carrying a message $\vec{e}(t) = (\cos 2\pi f t, \sin 2\pi f t)$ that is represented by a harmonic oscillator which vibrates with frequency f (representing the "color" of the light). The internal oscillator is used as a clock to encode the time of flight t, which depends on the source–detector distance. Think of this message as the hand of a clock that rotates with frequency f.

- Source: The source creates a messenger and waits until its message has been processed by the detector before creating the next messenger, so that there can be no direct communication between the messengers. When a messenger is created its time of flight is set to zero.

- Detector: We describe the model for one of the many identical detectors building up the detection screen. These detectors operate independently from each other. Detectors are very complex devices. In its simplest form, a light detector consists of a material that can be ionized by light. This produces a signal, which is amplified. In Maxwell's theory, the interaction between the incident electric field and the detector material is the result of a coupling of the oscillation of the incoming photon with the polarization of the detector material due to the photons that came in previously. In cases where incoming photon and remaining polarization are in phase—in the same state of oscillation—the detector is likely to click; in cases where they are out of phase, no click will occur.[4] If the "memory" of the detector is good enough and if there are enough messengers, the event-based simulation generates the interference pattern

---

4   In more detail: the interaction between the incident electric field $\vec{E}$ and the detector material takes the form $\vec{P} \cdot \vec{E}$, where $\vec{P}$ denotes the polarization vector of the material. In the case of a linear response of the material $\vec{P}(\omega) = \chi(\omega)\vec{E}$, where χ denotes the electric susceptibility of the material and ω is the frequency of the impinging monochromatic light wave. In the time domain this relation expresses the fact that the material retains some memory about the incident electric field, $\chi(\omega)$ representing the memory kernel. In the discrete-event model, the kth message in the form of the two-dimensional vector $\vec{e}_k(t) = (\cos 2\pi f_k t)$ is taken to represent the elementary unit of electric field $\vec{E}(t)$. The electric polarization $\vec{P}(t)$ of the material is represented by a two-dimensional vector $\vec{p}_k$. Upon receipt of the kth message by the processor modeling the detector this vector is updated according to the rule $\vec{p}_k = \gamma \vec{p}_{k-1} + (1 - \gamma)\vec{e}_k$ where $0 < \gamma < 1$ and $k > 0$. After updating the vector $\vec{p}_k$, the processor uses the information stored in this vector to decide whether to generate a "click." As a highly simplified model, we let the processor generate a binary output signal S_k using the intrinsic threshold function $S_k = \Theta(\vec{p}_k^2 - r_k)$, where $\Theta(\cdot)$ denotes the unit step function and $0 \leq r_k < 1$ is a uniform pseudo-random number. For $\gamma \to 1^-$ and a large enough number of messengers we recover the interference pattern from wave theory.

that we know from wave theory. This detector is a kind of adaptive machine that "learns" from the incoming entities.

The whole algorithm is very simple and does not require a lot of computer power: a personal computer suffices. Fig. 9 shows a comparison of the simulation results from about six million entities with the theoretical result $I(\theta) = A[\sin(^{(a\pi \sin \theta/\lambda)})/(^{(a\pi \sin \theta/\lambda)})]^2 \cos^2(^{(d\pi \sin \theta/\lambda)})$ obtained from a straightforward application of Maxwell's theory in the Fraunhofer regime. As can be seen, the agreement is excellent. The agreement is not only perfect for this parameter set but also for many others (Jin et al. 2010).

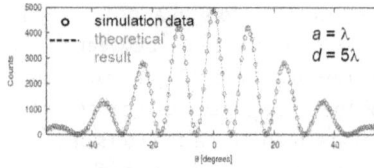

[Fig. 9] Detector counts as a function of the angular detector position as obtained from event-by-event simulations of the two-beam interference experiment depicted in Fig. 7. The sources, emitting particles, are slits of width $a = \lambda$ (λ = 670 nm), separated by a distance $d = 5\lambda$ and the source–detector distance $X = 0.05$ mm. A set of 1,000 detectors is positioned equidistantly in the interval [–57°, 57°], each of them receiving on average about 6,000 photons. In the simulation model $\gamma = 0.999$.

Multiple-Slit Experiment with Slit Device

We consider the interference experiments with two-slit and three-slit devices as depicted in Fig. 10. In contrast to the two-beam experiment, in these experiments not only interference but also diffraction occurs. In the discrete-event model of these experiments the rules for the photons and source are the same as the ones used to simulate the two-beam inter- ference experiment. As we may assume that in this case the multiple-slit device, and not the detectors, causes the diffraction and interference, the adaptive machines modeling the detectors are replaced by counters that simply count each incoming messenger.

An adaptive machine models the multiple-slit device. An entity follows the classical trajectory in the multiple-slit device thereby possibly transferring momentum to the multiple-slit device. Hence, the multiple-slit device is modified by the passing entity and as a result each passing entity expe- riences a slightly different multiple-slit device. Thus the multiple-slit device is a kind of adaptive machine that "learns" from the incoming entities.

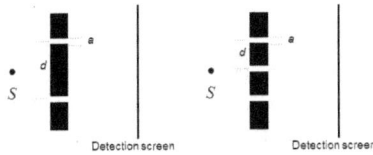

[Fig. 10] Setup for a single-entity experiment with a two-slit device (left) and a three-slit device (right).

Fig. 11 shows some simulation results for entities impinging on a two-slit device at normal incidence ($\theta = 0$) and under an angle of incidence ($\theta = 30°$). Also a result for a three-slit device on which entities impinge at normal incidence is shown. The simulation results are compared with the theoretical results in the Fraunhofer regime and again perfect agreement is found.

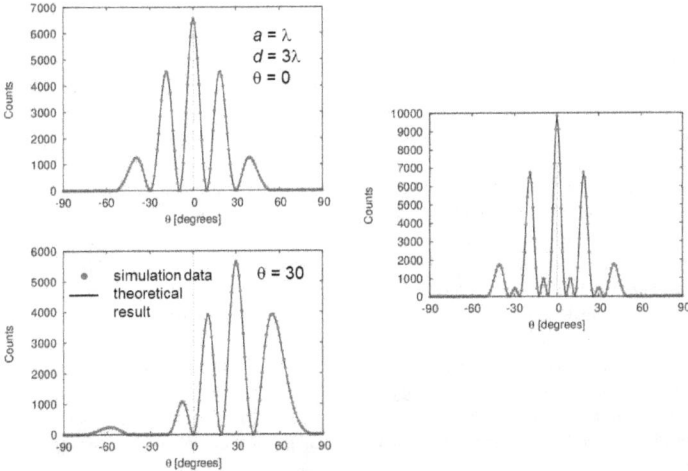

[Fig.11] Detector counts as a function of the angular detector position as obtained from event-by-event simulations of the multiple-slit interference experiments shown in Fig. 10. Left: Two-slit device, Right: Three-slit device.

Conclusions

The discrete-event simulation method models physical phenomena as chronological sequences of events. The events in the simulation are the action of an experimenter, a particle emitted by a source, a signal detected by a detector, a particle impinging on a material, and so on. These are the events that are extracted from a thorough analysis of how the experiment is performed. The next step, and this is the basic idea in the approach, is to invent an algorithm that uses the same kind of events (data) as in experiment and reproduces the statistical results of quantum or wave theory without making use of this theory. Discrete-event simulation successfully emulates single-entity experiments (so-called quantum experiments) demonstrating interference, entanglement, and uncertainty. By construction, the discrete-event approach is free of logical inconsistencies.

In principle, a kind of Turing test could be performed on data coming from a single-entity interference experiment performed in the laboratory and on data generated by the discrete-event simulation approach. This test would lead to the conclusion that both data sets look quite similar. The observer would be quite puzzled because this type of laboratory experiment is often classified as "quantum" yet no quantum theory is used in the discrete-event simulation.

References

Bach, Roger, Damian Pope, Sy-Hwang Liou, and Herman Batelaan. 2013. "Controlled double-slit electron diffraction." *New Journal of Physics* 15: 033018.

Ballentine, Leslie E. 2003. *Quantum Mechanics: A Modern Development*. Singapore: World Scientific.

Born, Max, and Emil Wolf. 1964. *Principles of Optics*. Oxford: Pergamon.

De Raedt, Koen, Hans De Raedt, and Kristel Michielsen. 2005. "Deterministic event-based simulation of quantum phenomena." *Computer Physics Communications* 171 (1): 19–39.

De Raedt, Hans, Fenping Jin, and Kristel Michielsen. 2012. "Event-Based Simulation of Neutron Interfermetry Experiments." *Quantum Matter* 1 (1): 20–40.

De Raedt, Hans, Kristel Michielsen, and Karl Hess. 2012. "Analysis of multipath interference in three-slit experiments." *Physical Review A* 85 (1): 012101.

De Raedt, Hans and Kristel Michielsen. 2012. "Event-by-event simulation of quantum phenomena." *Annalen der Physik* 524 (8): 393–410.

Einstein, Albert. 1949. "Remarks to the Essays Appearing in this Collective Volume." In *Albert Einstein: Philosopher-Scientist*, edited by Paul Arthur Schilpp, 663–688. New York: Harper & Row.

Feynman, Richard P., Robert Leighton, and Matthew Sands. 1965. *The Feynman Lectures on Physics*, Vol. 3. Reading, MA: Addison-Wesley.

Garcia, Nicolas, I. G. Saveliev, and M. Sharonov. 2002. "Time-resolved diffraction and interference: Young's interference with photons of different energy as revealed by time resolutions." *Philosophical Transactions of the Royal Society A* 360 (1794): 1039–1059.

Gähler, Roland, and Anton Zeilinger. 1991. "Wave-optical experiments with very cold neutrons." *American Journal of Physics* 59 (4): 316 - 324.

Jacques, Villain, E. Wu, T. Toury, F. Trenssart, A. Aspect, P. Grangier, and J-F. Roch. 2005. "Single-photon wavefront-splitting interference – An illustration of the light quantum in action." *The European Physical Journal D* (EPJ D) 35 (3): 561–565.

Jin, Fengping, Shengjun Yuan, Hans De Raedt, Kristel Michielsen, and Seiji Miyashita. 2010. "Corpuscular Model of Two-Beam Interference and Double-Slit Experiments with Single Photons." *Journal of the Physical Society of Japan* 79 (7): 074401.

Merli, Pier Giorgio, Gian Franco Missiroli, and Giulio Pozzi. 1976. "On the statistical aspect of electron interference phenomena." *American Journal of Physics* 44 (3): 306–307.

Michielsen, Kristel, Fengping Jin, and Hans De Raedt. 2011. "Event-Based Corpuscular Model for Quantum Optics Experiments." *Journal of Computational and Theoretical Nanoscience* 8 (6): 1052–1080.

Michielsen, Kristel, and Hans De Raedt. 2012. "Interference: Double-Slit." *Quantum Mechanics*, accessed June 4, 2017, http://www.embd.be/quantummechanics/double_slit.html.

Michielsen, Kristel, and Hans De Raedt. 2014. "Event-based simulation of quantum physics experiments." *International Journal of Modern Physics C* 25 (8): 1430003.

Stephan, Michael, and Jutta Docter. 2015. "JUQUEEN: IBM Blue Gene/Q® Supercomputer System at the Jülich Supercomputing Centre." *Journal of Large-Scale Research Facilities* 1: A1.

Tonomura, Akira, J. Endo, T. Matsuda, T. Kawasaki and H. Ezawa. 1989. "Demonstration of single-electron buildup of an interference pattern." *American Journal of Physics* 57 (2): 117–120.

Tonomura, Akira. 1998. *The Quantum World Unveiled by Electron Waves*. Singapore: World Scientific.

Walia, Arjun. 2015. "The Top 3 Mind-Boggling Quantum Experiments That Will Drop Your Jaw," Collective Evolution, accessed June 4, 2017, http://www.collective-evolution.com/2015/08/01/the-top-3-mind-boggling-quantum-experiments-that-will-drop-your-jaw/.

Wolfram, Stephen. 2002. *A New Kind of Science*. Champaign, IL: Wolfram Media.

Zeilinger, Anton, Roland Gähler, C.G. Shull, Wolfgang Treimer, and Walter Mampe. 1988. "Single- and double-slit diffraction of neutrons." *Reviews of Modern Physics* 60 (4): 1067–1073.

Zeilinger, Anton. 1999. "Experiment and the foundations of quantum physics." *Reviews of Modern Physics* 71 (2): S288–S297.

Discussion with Kristel Michielsen and Hans De Raedt

Eric Winsberg: So, I have two questions—one quick sort of specific question and a more general one. The quick question is: there was this experiment done a couple of months ago, I think, which claimed it closed the Einstein–Podolsky–Rosen (EPR) loopholes or whatever. Can you guys do that within your paradigm here?

Kristel Michielsen: We have simulated EPR experiments, yes.

EW: But the one that was just done a couple of months ago, that supposedly closed the loopholes or whatever?

KM: There are two different approaches. On the one hand we can simulate various experiments. For this particular experiment we have to study how to implement it. That's one thing. On the other hand there is a fundamental problem with this type of experiment and for us it doesn't matter whether all the loopholes are closed or not because there will always be one remaining. That's simply because one cannot perform the thought experiment as it was originally designed. Hence, these are two different things. But if one performs an Einstein–Podolsky–Rosen–Bohm (EPRB) experiment and finds a violation of a Bell-type inequality then we can simulate it. For example, we have simulated the single-photon EPRB experiment performed by Gregor Weihs in Vienna. We have also simulated the EPR experiment with neutrons. So those two EPR experiments we already simulated—but of course, people come with more and more experiments.

EW: Okay, here's my more sort of philosophical question. There are a number of ways of thinking about what the puzzles in quantum mechanics are. One way of thinking about it that I sort of find useful is that what seems to be wrong in a way with the conventional presentation of quantum mechanics is that it gives us two different laws of evolution. It says there's the time-dependent Schrödinger equation, which evolves the wave function until you measure it and then there is a collapse. Why is there a collapse when you measure it? What's so special about measurement? Shouldn't measurement be described by the same theory that describes the evolution of the rest of the world? Why do measurement devices obey different laws than the rest of the world? It seems to me that one necessary condition for having a kind of adequate foundational story about what's going on in quantum mechanics is to not have that difference between how the world behaves and how detectors behave. But it seems to be built into your way of doing things that there...

KM: There's no difference. In our approach there is no difference between the detectors and all the...

EW: But don't you have different rules for entities and detectors and such? I thought that was kind of the...

KM: No, because...

EW: I mean, one way of thinking about it is this: in a way, whatever kind of representational system one has for the world, whether it's differential equations or event simulations or whatever it is, what one would like at the end of the day is one theoretical apparatus for quantum systems and for measurement systems and not to treat them separately.

KM: But in our approach they are not treated separately. We are always designing consistent models. It depends a little bit on the experiment you're looking at. Sometimes we encounter an experiment for which we have to build in new features. This could be a new apparatus for example, or it can be like as shown here, in the two-beam and two-slit experiment. In the case that you only have two sources and a detector, the detector has to be special, you could say. It needs to have some rules.

If we have this other device between the source and the detector, this two-slit device, then we can say that this two-slit device plays a special role and that we can take a very simple detector, which is simply counting every incoming entity. What we mean by saying that the simulation model has to be consistent is that if we take our more complex detector and put it behind the two-slit device, we can still obtain an interference pattern. The idea is that we cannot know beforehand how complicated the device needs to be for simulating all kinds of experiment. Another very simple example is a beam splitter. One can make the model very simple, and say I observe 50% of the entities is going left and 50% is going right—I can just put a random number generator in place of the beam splitter: half is going left and half is going right. Fine. If one is going to make a Mach-Zehnder interferometer with this type of beam splitter, it's not going to work. In that case one needs something more complex for the beam splitter.

From then on we use the more complex model for the beam splitter and use it to construct other experiments. We do the same in modeling other devices. So what we do is make a toolbox. We want the toolbox to be consistent. In the end the toolbox should be such that if one is designing an experiment one should be able to say I need this and this and this apparatus, so I go to the toolbox and take all the corresponding components, put them together, and simulate the experiment. That is our approach. In that sense there is no big difference between simulation and experiment. We make no distinction between classical and quantum. By the way, one can indeed say that one should include the detector in the quantum theoretical description. One can do that no problem because then one has one big quantum system. But, this does not solve the problem. Quantum theory describes the whole system, the whole experimental setup, including in principle the detector. But, it does not help, where does one stop?

Hans De Raedt: So, I think the final problem is the event. One has to explain the event. The fact that our brain somehow registers an event means that in the end one has to put a measurement system in our brain, if one goes with this logic of always extending quantum theory to incorporate more and more and more.

EW: Right, I mean there are various approaches to this, one is to think that if you get enough stuff in the same place it collapses as a law or, you know...

HDR: There are difficulties there. So if you say the collapse, we have to evoke the collapse, then the collapse is outside of quantum theory. The formula is not quantum theory, it's something external. It's fine, but in the end if you do the logic you have to say everything collapses in my brain. Not only in yours but also in mine. In everyone's brain. Of course we can believe that, but the question is not whether it's true or not: the question is whether there is a more rational explanation to it.

Lukas Mairhofer: Let's put it this way, Karen Barad tells us that Niels Bohr told us that if you look at an interference experiment you somewhere have to make a cut between your observed system and your observing system. Where you make the cut is kind of arbitrary but it determines what the result of your observation will be. For me, what you told us so much resembles this that for me it's really hard to believe that you treat quantum systems and classical systems alike. Because you showed us that the adaptive system can be the screen or the diffraction element, and I would claim that it should be possible to make the entity the adaptive system. Just that you're able to change the functions of different parts of your experimental system—isn't that something that is so inherently quantum and that is so much not there in the classical world?

KM: First of all I would say there is no quantum world and there is no classical world. The only thing we can do is give a description of the world. This way of describing is just the same technique I use here to simulate these so-called quantum experiments. One is always talking about quantum experiments but the question is, are they really quantum? What does it mean? So, that's another question. Actually, using the same methods and apparatuses we simulate classical optical systems. We can simulate the Brewster angle single photon by single photon. Where then is the quantum?

LM: But can you do it with classical billiard balls like atoms?

KM: Yes. On the computer we can. But these are just simple models for what is going on. It gives a description in terms of...

LM: I think my problem is that I have the feeling that your whole epistemic approach is not classical. Because ascribing these adaptive functions, or being able to ascribe this adaptiveness to an arbitrary part of the system, is already something where the line between the observer and the object is getting so blurred and so on that in a Newtonian world this somehow feels very awkward for me. But okay.

KM: Okay. Hans De Raedt, do you have a comment?

HDR: What's so special about Newton?

LM: I just want to say that to me it seems that it's not Newtonian. It's not the classical epistemic approach.

HDR: Yes, but don't mix classical with Newton. Of course it's not classical Hamiltonian.

KM: It's not Hamiltonian mechanics, but in a sense it's maybe better to think outside of physics like for the other examples I have given. It's a methodology applied to physics but maybe it's less strange if you forget about...

LM: I don't find your approach strange. I just would find it strange to link this approach to a classical epistemic world view where there is a strict separation of the observer and the observed system. Because what you described is so completely different from that. That's all I wanted to say.

Mira Maiwöger: If you would want to simulate an experiment that throws apples through two slits, what would you need to change in order to get the two Gaussian probability distributions overlapping? The distribution that one can observe when one throws lots of apples through two slits?

KM: This is also a matter of dimensions and parameter values. If we do these two slit experiments, think about the dimensions. We have these rules and then it still fits.

HDR: In this particular case you just turn off the adaptiveness of the machine. That's it. Then it simply makes straight trajectories. In a sense you turn off the interaction of the entity and the slit.

KM: You have this parameter gamma there, so you have a range of possible values. If one goes to the wave description then we take gamma close to one and otherwise close to zero...

HDR: That is also what it is in Feynman's picture: it thinks of bullets going through the slit and the bullet and the slit. I mean one could take away the slit and just shoot the bullet in a narrow region and one would have the same answer. So, if we do this in the simulation, say switch off the interaction between the slit and the object, then bullet behavior is observed. So, essentially that is the rule. If one removes the adaptiveness it behaves as classical Hamiltonian mechanics.

Stefan Zieme: I think I have the same question that has been asked several times before—just to be sure that I got it right. You have a local description of your entities in your simulation? My first question would be how do you cope with Bell's inequality, and didn't you just shift everything you did into the detector? That would be my first thought. If you didn't, how would you then cope with Bell's inequality? I would find that rather strange, especially in regard of your EPR–Bohm experiment, because it's hard to see what you are simulating—that would be the first question that comes to my mind. If you talk about local entities in your simulation I have the impression you just shifted the problem to the detector. By training I have to say this; it's not that I'm convinced of it, but my training...

KM: You have to ask this question. Then I would say it's hard to ask about simulating Bell's inequality experiment, because we really have to see how this experiment is performed.

SZ: Like I think Clauser in 1972 was the first one to come up with this idea. I don't know anything about that, only very little. But I wondered how yours compares with that one?

KM: I will tell you what the most important ingredients are. We all have in mind the thought experiment of EPR, so a source sending pairs of particles. One particle is going to the left, the other one is going to the right. If one is up then you detect the other one as down. So that's one thing, but now one is going to do an experiment. This situation is not so ideal because one has to, in the end, identify pairs. If one looks closely at the experiments, it depends on how it's done, but in most of them time is needed in order to determine whether the particles belonged to a pair. So, there is some coincidence time needed in order to determine whether one has pairs. This already tells one that if one does a simulation, time is an important ingredient, which is not present in quantum theory. One then has to see how to simulate the experiment as the experimenters do it. This also means that one has to do the data analysis in the same way as the experimenters do it. What they do is choose a certain time window themselves. If we include all these ingredients in our simulation then although we have a local method, we correlate the data based on time stamps and by comparing time differences to a time window. So…

HDR: Maybe I may add here. In this particular case, this is the simplest simulation you can do from our perspective in the sense that you do not even need adaptive machines for it. So the only thing you have to do is…

KM: Is you have a source.

HDR: One has the source. One looks at what the experiment really entails, not at some idea that people have about the experiment. One really looks at how the experiment is being done, one puts all these things together, and one makes a simulation of it and it simply reproduces everything.

KM: In this case it's simple. You have a source emitting pairs and you have a detector that simply counts. Everything is counted.

SZ: So you will measure something that is bigger than two?

HDR: Absolutely.

SZ: And you have a local description? There's something contradictory. I don't know where to put the contradiction yet for me.

KM: No, it's even stronger. What we observe is a correlation that exactly corresponds to the one of the singlet state. So we do not only find a violation, but it is two times the square root of two. Another thing that we find, and which is usually not shown in the experiment, is that the single particle expectation value is zero and does not depend on the setting.

EW: So this is just by way of giving you a little bit of an idea of what might be going on here. There's a sort of long tradition of studying the Bell-type experiments by looking at the detector efficiency. If you rule out the assumption—all the analyses of these experiments relies on the assumption that when the detectors fail to detect that's a random event—if you give that up, you have a lot of wiggle room, and something like that is going on here I assume, but I'm not sure.

KM: Some filtering is going on, which...

HDR: Mathematically speaking, everybody refers to Bell's inequality but one can also look at the experimental situation, which by necessity requires measurement of times. Then generalize Bell's inequality to this situation. The inequality changes and this new inequality one can never validate—never. The limit is not two, the limit is four. This has been done by many people, but it's hardly mentioned in literature. So nobody seems to care.

KM: So one has to look at the correct inequality.

Martin Warnke: I would like to ask a question to everybody, not just the two of you. Could all this puzzlement we're now experiencing collectively, could that stem from the fact that we are newly coming down from the Platonic heaven of ideas to a very, very concrete description of what's actually happening? Could that be the media effect that we always look for? Might computer simulations have in this case the effect that you could deviate from very tough idealizations to a very concrete description? Might that be the difference? It seems that to me, but I'm not sure about it.

HDR: I certainly agree. I think as KM said the basic starting point is perception, not some idea we have about the world.

KM: So, not a mathematical model that is already based on many assumptions and simplifications.

MM: My question is could you have conceived a Bell experiment if not for this ideal, if not for these ideas of quantum physics? Could this experiment have been done? I think it's an interaction of course; this description is really concrete, but would there be experimental evidence of a Bell-type experiment without the idea of quantum physics being there?

HDR: If I remember the history of Bell's work well, Bell set up this inequality to prove quantum theory wrong, not to prove it right. So... no, no... that is what was made afterwards.

KM: Afterwards, not originally.

HDR: Bell was a strong believer in Bohmian theory and he wanted to show, that was his intention, he wanted to show that quantum theory was wrong. The experiment turned out to violate the inequality and then people started to change... you can look up the history. This has been lost somehow.

EW: You're right that Bell was a Bohmian, that's absolutely right, but Bohm's theory is nonlocal and so what Bell was out to prove was that there couldn't be a local rival to Bohmian mechanics.

HDR: Maybe we're not going to discuss these kinds of things.

Arianna Borrelli: I just wanted to say something on the subject of this media effect. I think here you can really see the power of a very powerful medium—mathematical formalisms. Because here the whole discussion in my opinion has very strongly been framed in terms of quantum mechanics versus classical mechanics. Is it the equations of quantum mechanics or the classical ones that are true? This is actually, from what I understood from the work that was presented here, not the point. This is more like you have the experiment, you have the perception. We have some clicks. We have some different mathematical formulas. Quantum mechanics, also classical mechanics, but that's not relevant in this context. Then we had maybe something else, something different, computer simulation. And this is the tension that is being presented here. I think it's sometimes difficult to approach, to frame the question in these terms, without immediately jumping and looking at what other mathematical formalisms are there. Of course all of these discussions could not have come up without quantum theory being there. That's clear—it would be crazy. That's not the issue, I just wanted to highlight this.

KM: Indeed, I agree. There is too much classification into classical, quantum, but we only look for an explanation or for a description so to speak. That's the only thing. Indeed.

3

Observing the Unobservable: Quantum Interference of Complex Macromolecules

Lukas Mairhofer

In my laboratory I work on a Kapitza–Dirac–Talbot–Lau interferometer for large and complex molecules. In this interferometer we have demonstrated the quantum interference for the largest objects that have shown quantum interference so far—well, at least we claim it's quantum interference. Those were molecules with a mass of more than 10,000 atomic mass units, which is about the mass of more than 10,000 hydrogen atoms. The interference pattern that we get looks like that shown in the inset of Fig. 1.

It is quite different from the patterns that we saw in the last talk. I will explain the reason for the difference in a second. This pattern is basically obtained by using an additional grating as a detection mask that is scanned over the molecular beam.

Our experimental setup is shown in Fig. 1. It is an interferometer that works with three gratings. The first grating is our source grating, which creates the coherence of our matter waves. We need the source grating because these matter waves are produced by simply heating a sample of the molecules using a very crude method, namely a ceramic cylinder around which we wrap some heating wire. They leave this oven through a slit and enter the vacuum chamber with a thermal velocity distribution, so they are everything but coherent. They never actually become coherent in the forward direction because we just cut out something like 20% of the velocity spread. But what we really need for seeing interference is spatial coherence, that is coherence transverse to the direction of the propagation of the molecules. This coherence is obtained by putting the first grating in the way of the molecular beam, and each opening, each slit of the grating, now acts as something like a point source. After this grating, the matter wave with which we describe the center of mass motion of our molecules coherently illuminates a few nodes of the second grating. This second grating in our case is not a material grating anymore, but it is created by retroreflecting a laser from a mirror such that it forms a standing light wave.

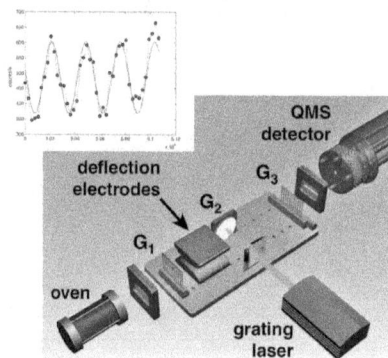

[Fig. 1] This sketch shows the main components of the setup of the Kapitza–Dirac–Talbot–Lau interferometer for matter waves. The molecules emanate from a crucible and form a molecular beam that passes three gratings and finally is ionized and detected. The inset shows the measured interference pattern, a sine-like modulation of the count rate that results when the third grating is scanned over the molecular beam (Source: Tüxen et al. 2010, 4145–4147).

So you see, in earlier times people diffracted light at matter; we now diffract matter at light. This works in the following way: the standing light field produces a periodic electromagnetic potential. In this electromagnetic potential the electrons are shifted inside the molecules. This induces a dipole moment in the molecule and this dipole moment then again interacts with the electromagnetic potential.

This interaction imprints a phase shift on the matter wave, induces in it a position-dependent shift of its momentum. As I already said, we use a third material mask of the same period to scan over the molecular beam, and behind this grating we ionize the molecules and count them in a quadrupole mass spectrometer.

You need a very good vacuum to see the interference effects. When the molecules interact with background gas on their way, you will loose your interference contrast. The actual setup is something like three meters long and is much emptier than many parts of the solar system, which contains a lot of dust and dirt. The reason why this pattern looks like such a nice sine curve is that we perform our experiments not in the far field, which was described in the talk before, but in the near field. Fig. 2 shows the transition between these two regimes, the near and the far field.

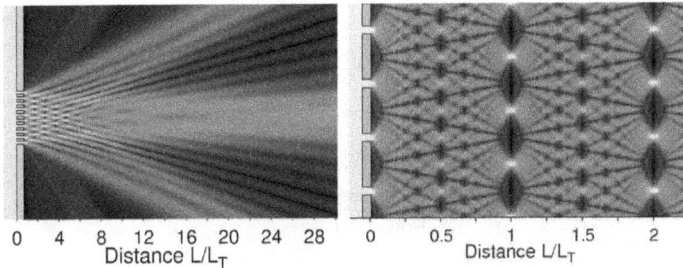

[Fig. 2] Left hand: Transition from the near to the far field. Right-hand picture shows a numerical simulation of the Talbot carpet (Source: Hornberger et al. 2012, 157–173).

You see that behind these narrow openings of the diffraction grating the waves evolve in a very chaotic way. You cannot really solve analytically what is happening there. But from all this chaos a certain order arises when at certain distances the pattern of the diffraction mask is reproduced, and this distance is the so-called Talbot distance. Also, you can see that at half the distance the pattern is reproduced with twice the period and so on. The structure that evolves here is sometimes called a Talbot carpet. On the right hand picture of Fig. 2 you see how the near field transits into the far field; this is not a sharp transition and where it happens depends on how many slits the diffraction mask has. In each Talbot order the outermost maxima of the pattern evolve into the far field. The number of slits determines how often the grating mask is reproduced, that is, how many Talbot orders you will see.

So, we put our detector somewhere in the second Talbot order, where you see a reproduction of the diffraction grating, and that is why you see such a nice sine curve here—because the potential of the standing light wave is a sine in the first order. Of course when I came to this conference I asked myself is this a computer simulation already? This fitting a sine curve into our data? I would say it is, but I'm not sure. I'm not sure what a computer simulation is exactly. Well, one thing for sure that my predecessors on the experiment did was asking the question about whether this diffraction pattern that we see really is a quantum diffraction pattern. Or is it just the result of classic ballistic diffraction, like of footballs hitting the goal post? They did a simulation where they compared how the visibility, the contrast of your interference pattern, would behave for different laser powers and the result are shown in Fig. 3.

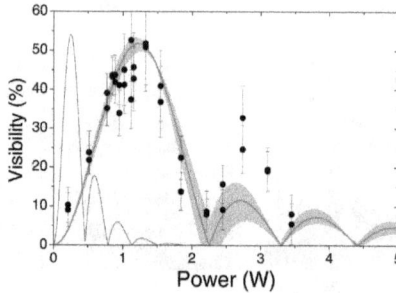

[Fig. 3] Fringe visibility as function of diffraction laser power. Measured data compared to simulation for classical and quantum interference (Source: Hornberger et al. 2012, 157–173).

The blue line gives you the development of the visibility for a classical theory and the red line gives you the predictions of quantum theory; you can see that the experimental results agree quite well with quantum theory, but definitely do not agree with a classical approach.

However, although we heat up about half a gram of molecules in our oven and many thousands of molecules are flying through the grating at the same time, what we see is not interference of molecules with one another, but of each molecule with itself. We claim that it has to be interference of the molecule with itself because the molecules are very hot. They have many internal degrees of freedom, many hundred degrees of freedom. It's very unlikely that two of the molecules are in the same state at the moment they are simultaneously passing through the grating. If they are not in the same state, they can be distinguished—and two distinguishable objects can not coherently interfere with each other. So what we see is the interference of molecules with themselves. But there is something really puzzling going on: interference should be something that only happens to waves. One has to be very careful to be clear that what we are looking at in our theoretical models is the center-of-mass wave function. It is a wave function that describes the motion of the center-of-mass of a really big object, and the wavelength is actually orders of magnitude smaller than the object. It doesn't tell us what happens to the components of the object, and we can interact with the object as if it was a complex particle with an inner structure. For example, we can measure the distribution of charges inside the molecule. Actually, when I told you that the light grating works because charges are shifted inside the molecules, I was using a particle picture to describe the diffraction of a wave. This is really weird to me, and it is also really weird to me that we can use the interference to probe the particle properties of the molecules, such as their electric polarizabilities or their permanent magnetic moment. These are properties that result from the internal structure of the molecules and that are not really part of my wave picture of these entities.

We can also do absorption spectroscopy in our interferometer—we send photons into the chamber, where they cross the molecular beam. When their wavelength is resonant with a transition in the molecules, they absorb the photon and get a kick to the side. While the matter wave is delocalized transverse to the direction of its center-of-mass motion, an absorption event takes place that is much more localized in the direction of this motion itself. In a way what happens in the experiment is something very strange, because we have a localized absorption of a photon by a molecule that is actually undergoing an interference process with itself. So it should be delocalized, and it is indeed delocalized in one direction and localized in the other direction.

References

Hornberger, Klaus, Stefan Gerlich, Philipp Haslinger, Stefan Nimmrichter, and Markus Arndt. 2012. "Colloquium: Quantum interference of clusters and molecules." *Reviews of Modern Physics* 84: 157–173.

Tüxen, Jens, Stefan Gerlich, Sandra Eibenberger, Markus Arndt, and Marcel Mayor. 2010. "Quantum interference distinguishes between constitutional isomers." *Chemical Communications* 46 (23): 4145–4147.

Discussion with Lukas Mairhofer

Eric Winsberg: Just a quick question about the comment you made about how it's weird that you're treating the molecule as a wave function, but then it has all these internal degrees of freedom that matter. Is that different from when you use an electron? After all, you might just look at the spin of the electron, which is a very reduced representation of it in respect to the electron's degrees of freedom. Maybe it's made up of some...

Lukas Mairhofer: Well, you don't have this many degrees of freedom in an electron so it's easier, or think of photons.

EW: Let's try electrons, right? You could look at an inner structure of an electron.

LM: Supposedly an electron is a point-like particle that has no inner structure. Of course you can prepare atoms in different states but it's easy to prepare them in the same state. It's really, really hard to do that with large molecules.

EW: What is the molecule that you're looking at?

LM: Well our working horse molecule is the fullerene C60; it consists of 60 carbon atoms and looks like a football with its round shape and the structure made up of pentagons and hexagons. But we use many other molecules, some tailor-made by chemists, some just as they exist, for example in biological systems. Right now we're doing interference with vitamins A, K, H and D. We are trying to show interference with longer chains of peptides and proteins, in the future maybe with a viroid. So those are the molecules we are working on. They are large enough to be called Schrödinger's cats, definitely, yes—it's really hard to prepare two cats in the same state.

Stefan Zieme: I guess the size of the molecule—I mean, how big can they be? It's just a question of how good the vacuum is so can you make an estimate on how far you can go and if you can make an estimate about whether it converges? What is the boundary between classical and quantum?

LM: That's a very interesting question, and that of course is a question that also drives us because it is at the foundations of physics. First of all it's not only a question of the vacuum... your de Broglie wavelength, that is, the wavelength of your matter wave, scales inversely with your mass, so your de Broglie wavelength becomes very small when your mass increases, and then to see the interference effect your interferometer needs to become very long. If you want to build an interferometer for a viroid, for the RNA strand without its protein shell, with the sources and the techniques that are available at the moment, it will be something like… each arm will be something like one or one and a half meters long. At the moment in our interferometer each arm is 10 centimeters long. Of course you need a good vacuum then. Also vibrations really become a problem when you have such a long interferometer. Even in the interferometer that I work on now you loose half of your contrast if your grating period is misaligned by half an Angström, that is half the radius of a hydrogen atom, for example because your laser wavelength has changed or something like that. So things like this are limiting you in a technical way. And then on the fundamental level, some theories claim that there is a limit on the size of the objects that you can show interference with. Because the question is, why do we not see quantum effects like interference in our everyday experience? Why does the world we live in seem to follow such a radically different physics? There are many approaches to explain this, and one is to claim that there is a spontaneous collapse of the wave function under its own gravity, for example. That would scale with the mass of the particle. Early spontaneous collapse models derived that you shouldn't see interference above 2,000 atomic mass units. Then it was about 10,000 atomic mass units, now it's about 100,000 atomic mass units. So there are some parameters you can tweak, but it seems that you cannot tweak them arbitrarily. At some point this model can be ruled out and this we try to test in our interference experiments.

EW: I mean in the Ghirardi–Rimini–Weber (GRW) theory, it depends on time. You can have an arbitrarily large thing not collapse, according to GRW, for a very short period of time.

LM: Yes. We look at it at reasonably long times, a few milliseconds.

Martin Warnke: I have a question because you yourself put up so many doubts and spoke of your puzzlement—my biggest puzzlement is having seen you with your young colleague in the laboratory, filling in that blue stuff at the left-hand side of the experimental system. Using a spoon, taking lumps of C60 atoms out of a box, putting them into the oven. Then you closed the apparatus and drew a very high vacuum. After that preparation in the real world with real and hard matter, then in the world of an isolated apparatus you perform an experiment that you describe as one where matter waves interfere with themselves. The blue material from the beginning transforms, or should I say, trans-substantiates, into uncorporal waves. How do you do that in your mind? Say in one quarter of an hour you're putting blue stuff into the left-hand side and after a few hours, when the vacuum is up again, you're thinking of matter waves. How do you do that?

LM: I asked that myself for a very long time, until after a bottle of red wine I thought of myself in a space suit drifting through a dark universe without any point of orientation and without any interaction, without any stars around me. Completely blind, completely isolated. I thought I might well think of myself as being delocalized then. What is the meaning of being localized when there is no frame of reference? When there is nothing you can map your location to, if there is no interaction with your environment? I think even in our human minds, we could imagine being delocalized—or at least the concept of being localized would lose its meaning.

Hans-Jörg Rheinberger: I have a little problem with the probes that you're using. So if you're using that fullerene, it somehow makes sense. But if you think of a protein, that usually only exists with a lot of water molecules around it and so on and so forth. So what do you do to these molecules before you shoot them into the vacuum and what happens to them in the vacuum?

LM: Proteins are not very happy in a vacuum, that is true. The proteins unfold, so they spread out. But for example, the aim with the virus would of course be to show that it is still reproductive afterwards and it is still this half-living thing that it was before. It's actually this transition between the gas phase and the in vivo environment that interests us so much. We try to attach water molecules to the protein in a controlled manner after we evaporate it, to see how that changes its behavior in the interferometer, its absorption of light and so on. To give you an example that is not a protein but that will make it clear why this is interesting, consider retinal, the molecule in your eye that triggers the visual process when it absorbs a photon. You know that you have different cells for blue light, for green light, and for red light. But the interesting thing is that it's always the same retinal in these cells. The shift in the absorption line is only caused by the protein that it has bonded to. It would be really interesting for biologists and chemists to know where retinal absorbs when it is alone, when it is in the gas phase, and nobody knows because you cannot resolve it with classic methods—only the sensitivity of our interference patterns will allow us to measure that.

Kristel Michielsen: Maybe I missed it, but how many molecules do you have in your interferometer?

LM: Our detection efficiency is lousy. We detect one in ten thousand to one in a million of the molecules arriving at the detector. When you run the interferometer, when you run a scan, you have something like 300, or okay, let's say you have something between 100 counts to 1,000 counts per second, but you can multiply this by a reasonably large number to get the actual number of molecules we have flying in there. The time of flight through the interferometer is a few milliseconds.

KM: So you have a bunch of molecules that goes at the same time?

LM: Yes, but they are distinguishable, they are not in the same state. So that at least in the quantum mechanical description you cannot make them interfere with one another.

Arianna Borelli: Of this question of the interference, because it was not very clear to me, what you meant that they cannot interfere if they are not in the same state, maybe you can make that clear, but now another question came to me. You speak always of waves, as far as I can tell, and never of fields. Of course if you would think of fields you would think there's this molecule field with different waves on it and then of course they might interfere with each other, waves in the same field— and now, moving into the mathematical world: if I think of these waves and waves in a field then they can all interfere. If you had to talk about fields, now speaking again in the mathematical world, would you say each of these waves is a different field or does that not make sense? As I said this is a former problem, but it's interesting for me to understand what you mean by interference and waves.

LM: The question of the field is very difficult for me because I have never seen a quantum field theory description for such huge molecules. I also have to admit that for this question I'm a little bit too much on the experimental side. As far as I see in the theory, I don't find an approach for a field theoretical model for what we do—just because the particles are too complicated. And yes, for the description of the center of mass motion you have a wave function.

AB: So you have a wave and, maybe I can put it in a more concrete way, these waves are waves in space and each particle has its own space? Its own space variables? Okay?

LM: Yes.

MW: May I quote Markus Arndt, the head of the group? When we talked to him he said there is actually no applicable theory for this situation and that we tried to measure what could not yet be calculated. Which is a very interesting point of view. Just a quote.

Anne Dippel: Hans, Kristel, what Lukas shows here right now, that's something you could model, but then this is not a simulation. You can't calculate it without a field theory.

LM: Yes, that's great. Isn't the simulation something you always can calculate?

MW: Maybe an analog simulation. I have just another question: You showed simulations but you didn't name them. So the graphics you used, as far as I know, are from the Duisburg group simulating the near fields. It's very peculiar for me. I know that your very highly esteemed colleagues in Duisburg are doing this, but why is this always something mute and invisible in your work? Why are there computer simulations that are of extreme importance for the Talbot carpet, which come, as far as I remember from the papers I've read, from the simulations they do in Duisburg. Could you describe the relationship between the experimental work and the computer simulations that were done beforehand, which you never talk about?

LM: Actually that's a thing I really forgot, because at one point I thought, 'Oh nice—I'll put in this picture and then I'll tell you that's the result of a computer simulation.' Especially this Talbot carpet; it's a numerical simulation of one of my colleagues. But we have a very strong collaboration with the group in Duisburg that has been doing the theory for many years. One member of our group, who developed the theory for all of our interferometers, joined the Duisburg group after doing his PhD with us. So there are very strong links to them. For me...why I don't talk about that work has two reasons. The first is that I don't understand it completely and it's their work. It's hard for me to present it. The other thing is: for me, there is very much the question that I asked in the beginning. What is a simulation? Because what they are doing is of course, that they develop models. They do that together with us, and model what is going on in the interferometer. Then they write the model as MATLAB code for it and then they basically do a fit on our results for free parameters and they get a lot of information about our interferometer. Is this a simulation where you simulate what would happen in an experiment? No—it's a fit on existing data based on a model, and I don't know if this is a simulation—I just don't know it. It might well be that you call this a simulation; for me it is more a reconstruction of data.

Sonia Fizek: I actually wanted to ask you why can't you just go digital? Why do you need to do it the way you do it, and now you've kind of answered that. Maybe the simulation, you could call it a simulation the minute you can change variables. So let's say you have this problem with the length of the arm in a simulation: in a digital world you could just remove that variable and it is no longer there. So you kind of falsify things and maybe that's when you can talk about simulating stuff that is not 100% a reflection of reality in your lab. Maybe they do it?

LM: I agree, if you start to think ahead about what is going to happen if you do this and this, that for me would be a simulation. Exactly.

Hans de Raedt: In this picture you showed a grating that looked perfect, but I assume in your experiment it's quite different?

LM: Since the grating has been in there for something like eight or nine years, I'm afraid it really is far from perfect nowadays.

HDR: Let's say you get it from—I don't know who makes it…

LM: Nobody makes it anymore, that's the problem.

HDR: Let me rephrase it: when you first got it, what were the specifications of these—are these openings the same?

LM: The period of the material grating is 266 nanometers, the opening fraction is 40%, and all the openings are supposed to be the same; after eight years that might not be true anymore. But this material grating is not the diffraction grating that produces your interference pattern. So if we talk about the actual diffraction grating, we need to talk about the laser. This laser we can specify very, very well. We can measure its wavelength with femtometer precision and keep it stable to a few picometers. We can measure its power very accurately and we can look at the profile of the beam when it enters and when it leaves the chamber. This is all necessary because this is an incredibly important screw for us to tweak.

HDR: I understand that. So the grating that you call G1 and G3 is of course essential for what you get out—what goes in the interferometer and also what you detect. Not for the pattern but for the...

LM: It is important for creating good coherence, and if you don't create good coherence you don't see interference anymore. It is also actually critical that all slits should look more or less the same.

KM: In your picture you mentioned that one molecule is self-interfering?

LM: Yes, that's what we would claim.

KM: So if one molecule arises and if you are lucky because of the detection efficiency you see the spot, very localized. So now the next one comes. How is your picture at the end. Do you find stripes in an interference pattern?

LM: I would claim that interference is not something that you can ascribe to a single particle or a single wave. For me interference is an ensemble phenomenon. You cannot, you will never resolve the interference pattern of a single interfering entity. As you said, you need a lot of them to see the pattern and I don't have a problem with this.

KM: In your picture you have self-interference but you need many, so how do you provide this?

LM: Well, you need many entities that have been interfering with themselves. You describe an ensemble of entities that have been interfering with themselves—with themselves because they cannot interfere with the others. The concept of this self-interference is that the center of mass wave function gets split by at least two slits of your grating or nodes of your standing light wave. That it is...

KM: In a way that's a wave description of the ensemble. Not of one. How do you do this with one?

LM: Well how do you distinguish between the ensemble description and the description of one entity? You cannot get the ensemble if you don't have many "ones" and you cannot have any description of "the one" if you don't measure the ensemble. For me it's not possible to get one without the other. If you give a description of the ensemble, you give a description of all the entities in the ensemble but you do not describe the properties of the individual entities. You will never see these wave properties if you only look at the individual entity or event.

4

Simulating Patterns, Measuring Fringes: Simulating Matter with Matter

Mira Maiwöger

I'm working in the group of Jörg Schmiedmayer at the *Atominstitut* of the Technical University in Vienna. Like Lukas Mairhofer I am experimenting with matter waves in a lab. In this talk I focus on the aspect of simulation and show you some experiments where we simulate interference patterns in order to explain what's going on in our experiment or to reproduce the experimental observations. In my lab we work with ultra-cold atoms. We're basically doing the opposite of what Lukas does: we're cooling atoms down to almost zero temperature, where strange things happen.

At high temperatures, individual atoms will behave like billiard balls. The lower the temperature gets the lower the velocity of the atom becomes. At the same time the wavelength of the matter waves associated with the atoms increases up to a certain critical point where the interparticle spacing is the same as their de Broglie wavelength and the matter waves start to overlap, until at zero temperature all these atoms form a giant matter wave that can be described by a single wave function. This is called a Bose–Einstein condensate (BEC). So in my lab we're working with rubidium atoms and we are developing new tools to manipulate them, to create BECs, and to perform different experiments with them.

In many other groups ultra-cold atoms, especially in optical lattices, are used as analog quantum simulators, and I thought I should mention that in this symposium. Ultra-cold atoms in such lattices are used as model systems, as analog model systems. The idea is that they behave like certain other systems, for example as if they were a superfluid or a magnetic material. So that behavior is simulated instead of calculating what a magnetic material would do. These cold atoms are observed in order to get the answer to a very different problem. This was first proposed by Feynman in 1982, when he said let the computer itself be built of quantum mechanical elements that obey quantum mechanical laws. Once you're having those giant matter waves, those ultra-cold atoms that you can manipulate really precisely and that you can read out really precisely, you basically have an intrinsically quantum mechanical system that you can interrogate instead of the solid state that you want to know some answers about.

[Fig. 1] (Courtesy of the author).

However, in our lab we are doing something different with BECs. Fig. 1 shows our experiment. It basically looks like any other cold atom experiment. We have a single vacuum chamber where we prepare the BEC and do all the stuff we want to do with it, and then perform measurements just by taking photographs of these atomic clouds. On one side, hidden behind the shield, is all the optics we need to manipulate and prepare the atoms in the right state in order to be magnetically trapped. In contrast to the type of traps that only work with laser light, we trap our atoms in magnetic fields, and these fields are produced by wires on an atom chip. One of the main advantages of this atom chip is that it's a really stable and versatile device to prepare, control, and manipulate our BECs.

In our group there is more than one BEC experiment, but I will focus on my experiment. There are many things that we do with this setup and the one I'm going to talk about today is the so-called optimal control of the motional state of a quantum system. Here we are using optimal control theories, so we're calculating what we should do with this cloud of ultra-cold atoms in order for it to behave in a certain way, and I will tell you how this works in a minute.

Another thing that we've been studying recently is a phenomenon called population inversion, which we can simulate with our atoms. That mechanism is required for optical lasers. In our system the wave function is initially sitting in the ground state of the magnetic potential, but we can manage to get all the atoms—or at least a huge fraction of atoms—up to the first excited state of this potential. In this case collisions between the atoms will occur that produce correlated pairs of atoms with opposite momentum. This is in some way analogous to down-conversion in a nonlinear optical medium.

In this sense we can also analogously simulate the effects that take place in a very different medium with our cold atoms systems. We usually work with quasi one-dimensional BECs.

In my experiment I generate cigar-shaped BECs. Cigar-shaped means they are 100 times longer than they are wide. Therefore in many situations we can describe the behavior that we're seeing with one-dimensional theories, which makes it easier for theoretical physicists to explain what is going on. It also adds some other phenomena that you don't see in three-dimensional physics. It's really about playing around with a system that is artificially abstractified in some sense. With the complexity of this experimental apparatus we actually eliminate a lot of the effects that could mess up the nice theory we have for it. So we have a tool to probe rather simple models. Furthermore, we recently learned how to split one BEC, one of those cigar-shaped condensates, in a double-well potential. Then we can also do interferometry with it. In 2013, a Mach-Zehnder interferometer was implemented with such BECs. We have a lot of little projects around the development of new tools; it is basically a playground with toys for ultra-cold atoms. Now I want to get back to this optimal control story, which has mainly been done by my colleague Sandrine van Frank during her PhD, and about which she taught me a lot last year.

What we want to do is to move a fraction of the atoms really precisely out of the ground state into which we are cooling down the atoms, where we are condensing them. So in our initial state all the atoms are in the ground state of the harmonic potential, and we want to transfer a portion of the atoms to this first excited state with a high fidelity. This could be 10% of the atoms, this could be 50%, this could be 90%. We came up with a scheme for that, together with theoreticians who modeled and who simulated how to do this. We achieve this by displacing the condensate transversely, that is along the tightly confined axis. This is achieved by really special pulses and those pulses were optimized by our colleagues in Ulm. You need to do a model of your system, the simplest way to describe the BEC; in this case it is a formula we call the nonlinear Gross–Pitaevskii equation. It is a variant of the Schrödinger equation in the mean-field description.

This approach treats the entire wave packet consisting of many atoms as a single wave. Atomic interactions are ignored; they only appear in a density term. We also ignore the longitudinal axis of our elongated BEC, which is also the axis where finite temperatures play a role—so we consider our condensate to have zero temperature. Then we need some handle to manipulate our system, which in our project is the transverse displacement of the BEC. This allows us to transfer a portion of the atoms from the ground state into the excited state. What the theoreticians do is that they minimize some sort of cost function, which in this case is the fidelity or the infidelity. So you want to minimize the error you make when transferring a fraction of the atoms to this first excited state. You want to be as precise as possible. The theoreticians have developed an algorithm that takes the technical limitations of our experiment into account. We went to our collaborators and said we can do up to 20 kilohertz. That's what the device can do, we cannot do more. We cannot shake it any faster. They came up with the sort of pulses that are very close to the quantum speed limit, the fastest you could do according to quantum theory.

I will tell you in a second how they work and what you can learn from that. Let me come back to the experimental tools. As I mentioned before we use an atom chip. We have to slow down the atoms a lot, to velocities that would correspond to a temperature of a thousandth part of a degree above absolute zero. Only then can we actually trap them in those magnetic fields produced by the chip, but in principle you use a really small, really thin trapping wire. When we run a current through this wire, it produces a magnetic field that, together with an additional external magnetic field, creates the harmonic potential where atoms are trapped and finally condense into the ground state. I think I never mentioned that we use rubidium 87, so one of the most well-behaved species that there is for doing BECs. That's a common quote of my professor Jörg Schmiedmayer: he always says rubidium is so well behaved, it's easy. So these well-behaved atoms we trap usually in those cigar-shaped potentials as I told you before, so that they are one-dimensional, or quasi one-dimensional.

Another tool we have, which I think our group was the first to apply, is using those radio frequency wires, where we send oscillating currents through, which allows us to deform a trap. If we turn on those RF wires and we send a current through them, we can dress the trap and deform it until double-well potentials evolve. The final shape depends on the power we are sending through the RF wires. This is basically our tool to create quite arbitrary trap shapes. In the optimal control case I want to have an anharmonic trap because I want to have the first-level spacing different from the second-level spacing so that I'm really able to target only this first excited state and not excite my atoms up to all the other states.

Another important tool in our experiment is the device to look at our atoms. We have an imaging system where we release the atoms from the trap, and then they fall through a thin sheet of focused laser light after 46 milliseconds' of free flight. We then collect the fluorescent photons emitted by the atoms on a camera. This means that we only see images that are integrated over the direction of gravity. So of course we can never image the entire cloud. We image it in several shots, like resolving layer after layer, but every time we would need to make a new BEC. We just wait for a certain time and then switch our trapping fields off. The atoms will fall down and fall through the light sheet and we collect single images.

Then we integrate over this direction and just stack the images together, and then you actually see the pulse shaking the atoms as well, so it's not only after transferring the atoms to this first excited state but even during this transfer that we take images.

For the analysis, in order to know whether our shaking and bringing the atoms into a target state has worked, we apply a fitting procedure. Here we use again this Gross–Pitaevskii equation, idealized for zero temperature and the one-dimensional situation where we only take the transverse direction into account and ignore everything that happens along the extended axis. It turns out that in order for the equation to fit the result reasonably well we need to take at least three states into account, so more than we actually want to address in the experiment. We need to take at least the ground state, the first excited state, and the second excited state into account. We then compare the simulations on the basis of the Gross–Pitaevskii and compare this to our measurements.

So we've created a very artificial scenario that actually works quite well for a certain amount of time. Afterwards it gets fuzzy and starts to decay. But we can control our well-behaved atoms reasonably well with this technique.

So as I mentioned before, a simulation is about taming the future, which was the part I was talking about before. But simulation is also about explaining the past. Of course we wanted to know why the theory does not fit the results after a certain point. What are the reasons that after, I don't know, 10 milliseconds our model that we're using to fit our data is deviating so much from the data, where the agreement with the theory breaks down somewhere? In the meantime we started to look into different models or different ways of simulating our situation. We now use a Gross-Pitaevskii equation again, but we change it a bit. With the usual Gross-Pitaevskii equation for zero temperature this behavior would continue much, much longer: it would not decay after 20 milliseconds. Here we are trying to simulate the system for finite temperatures and we actually see that we can get there. So it's probably enough, at least for the first 20 milliseconds, just to add temperature to our model and we learn that this is the critical point that was missing before. So that is how I experience the interplay between theory and experiment.

Discussion with Mira Maiwöger

Anne Dippel: Thank you Mira for showing the opposite side of complex quantum systems, showing quantum behavior, and maybe there are some questions from the audience concerning that experiment? It's going in the opposite direction, it's another setup. Still, we have quantum mechanics proved.

Hans De Raedt: I have kind of a more general question. If I look at the sophistication of your experiment; it's really impressive by itself. To see what appears to be some quantum effect and then compare this to what people did in the 1800s looking at the spectra of simple atoms, which was of course the source for developing quantum theory. There is something strange. Originally to see quantum effects you had to do nothing: just look and it's really true. In the meantime in order to see something that even closely resembles a little bit quantum behavior you have to have extremely expensive equipment, very sophisticated things, tools—a lot of people working on it.

Mira Maiwöger: To be honest to me this is part of the fun, that my object of study is some piece of reality that to me feels so highly artificial. I mean it was predicted in 1925 and it took 70 years to produce it in a lab for the first time. I really enjoy that I'm actually studying this artificial thing that to some degree can be useful as well when trying to simulate other systems.

HDR: Yes, sure, I can definitely appreciate the fun, I see that too. My question goes a little bit further. The fact that you have to work so hard to see it also means something. It's not just fun.

MM: Of course it means something—we can create a very specific phenomenon that consists of 10,000 to 100,000 atoms. These atoms are a fact that lasts a few, 10, milliseconds—which is a rather long time scale for a fact describable by a single wave function.

HDR: Under the right conditions.

MM: Under the right conditions, yes.

HDR: So the only thing you're doing actually is...

MM: Creating the right conditions. Yes, yes.

HDR: But if quantum theory or quantum mechanics is supposed to be all around, it should not be necessary to wait for the correct conditions to be realized to see it. In the case of atoms, there's no doubt about it. That's clear. You don't have to produce spectral conditions, you'd see them right away. That there are lines are in the spectra and so on. But the more sophisticated we get, the more complicated the conditions are.

MM: Yes, what is reality?

Wolfgang Hagen: What is reality and what is the phenomenon and what is the difference in your experiment?

MM: I cannot separate. In my experiment I would say I cannot separate my phenomenon Bose–Einstein condensate (BEC) or this entity BEC from this huge apparatus.

WH: Does that mean that there is no difference between reality and phenomenon?

MM: No, because I make a cut between apparatus and object in describing it. By the way physicists deal with this phenomenon BEC we make this cut. We choose to decide that this tiny, tiny cloud of atoms out of this huge apparatus here is the object. We decide to describe only those 10,000 or 1,000 atoms that are prepared in such a way that they're consistently described by this theory. This is a cut I'm making. Of course I cannot separate my BEC from this huge apparatus that produces it. But in our way of thinking about it we can. Or we choose to do so. Or play with it and try to extend it and so on.

Arianna Borrelli: Thanks, yes, I'm working on the same issue. But more on the theoretical side. Because you speak of Bose–Einstein condensation, BEC, and then you referred of course to Einstein's paper, and of course in the Einstein paper the theory is half formal. What exactly he was writing there, it's a bit what we interpret from it. My question would be, your phenomenon—is it Bose–Einstein condensation and if so how is it primarily defined? Is it that equation for example? Of course the term Bose–Einstein condensation is something that you could apply to many, many other phenomena, to photons and so on. Is there for example some bridge through some theory or experiment between all those phenomena and your condensate? I'm trying to clarify how universal the idea of Bose-Einstein condensate is, because you talk about it as though it were universal and refer back to the Einstein paper, and of course I understand there is a problem with the experiment, but at the theoretical level is there universality?

MM: It really depends on the dimensionality of the condensate. I mentioned before that we were working with one-dimensional or quasi one-dimensional BECs, and if you treat the phenomenon of Bose–Einstein condensation theoretically in a stringent way then there is condensation only in three dimensions or in two dimensions. So in one dimension we always only can say condensed in a sense that we can claim that all the atoms are sitting in the ground state only in the transverse direction. Along the long axis of the BEC there are always phase fluctuations going on. Having a single wave function describing the condensate with a single phase does not work for the 1D case. We can, however, develop theories that can model how many phases we would need to describe the whole condensate and so on. I don't know—did this answer your question? No, it's not universal. Depending on the number of dimensions you have different scenarios, but you can describe them reasonably well to some degree until you get to a problem that you cannot describe anymore.

Lukas Mairhofer: I just wanted to come back to the discussion before. When I listen to Mira, I sometimes tell her you're not doing, you're not... well it's hard to say in English. You're looking at art, not at nature. You're looking at a piece of art. But in that way we can separate the artifacts, the drawing or whatever from the tools with which we made it. In that way I think we can make the cut, or we are allowed to make a cut, between Van Gogh's drawings and the palette that he used to make them.

AD: There is no difference between art and nature.

MM: Donna Haraway's slogan, "querying what counts as nature," is my categorical imperative.

AD: Not exactly, creating our own reality and the reflections about it that we discussed. This was the reason why I invited you and I'm very happy that this became very clear here, how artificial the experiment itself is.

MM: The nature of the experiment.

AD: The nature that is made within those experiments, compared to 200 years ago. Are there more questions?

Frank Pasemann: A last remark, that nature can be very strange.

AD: Yes, nature can be very strange, absolutely.

5

Event-Based Simulations: Is there a Need for New Physical Theories?

Frank Pasemann

Following the discussions concerning the role of computer simulations in the development of natural sciences, and especially for the physical sciences, at some point I was confronted with the statement that, as a result of these simulations, "there is a need for new theories in physics." For me as a theoretical physicist this was a quite provoking appraisal, which showed up, almost naturally, in the debate on the interpretation of quantum mechanical predications. Based on the papers on event-based simulations (see Michielsen and De Raedt 2014) it was argued that for explaining quantum phenomena, like, for instance, the interference patterns in electron-scattering experiments, no quantum theoretical assumptions have to be made. The specific type of the described computer simulations will reproduce results of quantum theory showing that there exist macroscopic, mechanical models of classical physics that mimic the underlying physical phenomena. This is in contrast with statements like, for instance, that of Richard Feynman saying that the double-slit experiment "is impossible, *absolutely* impossible, to explain in any classical way, and which has in it the heart of quantum mechanics" (see Feynman 1989).

As a first reaction to this situation I had to reformulate the statement in terms of the question, which gave the title of my talk. Then I had to reassure myself about what I am willing to understand by a theory, by a physical theory, and, on the other hand, what kind of ingredients are necessary for setting up significant computer simulations of physical systems.

So, what I would like to present here are some general remarks about what I think are basic properties of physical theories; to make sure that we are talking about the same thing when demanding something new. And because the topic of this workshop is the context of computer simulations, and especially the simulation of physical experiments, I would like to add some general comments on simulations used for research in natural sciences. So I will not go into the specific simulations, which were presented in the first talk, and it is only at the end of my talk that I will try to imbed their event-based simulations into the scheme I will introduce.

Let me start with a description of a physical theory. I will do that in terms of a few simple but strong statements. This view is influenced mainly by the situation at the end of what may be called "the Old Science," characterized by the state of theoretical physics around the 1970s when it was still able to predict, besides the outcome of quantum mechanical experiments, also the outcome of those in the high-energy domain. But I think with respect to quantum phenomena this view of an established theory is still valid.

Although this is trivial, if one wants to set up a new physical theory, or a new type of a theory, it should be clear in which domain of phenomena it should be placed. So the first statement will be: **Every physical theory describes a well-defined area of physical phenomena**.

There are of course different ways to identify such domains. For example, one may refer to the length scale, which is quite natural, and talk about subatomic or atomic phenomena, about the domain of everyday physics that is described by classical physics, or about phenomena on the cosmic scale.

One can also refer to the forces that dominate the physical processes in a certain domain, and one may distinguish between the physics of strong forces, of weak forces, of electromagnetic forces, and of gravitational forces. The scattering phenomena under consideration here are primarily related to the single particle phenomena in the atomic domain, that is, we are in the arena of quantum (field) theory.

At this point one should perhaps mention the observation that there is a large gap in existing theories concerning the number of particles involved in processes. We have very nice theories about single particles or single objects, and we can often handle systems with two objects quite nicely. For the other extreme (i.e., systems composed of very many particles) stochastic theories are very effective. Between these two extremes there is the interesting physics of "medium-sized" systems, which is difficult to describe in detail. Even when dealing with just three objects the classical theories get into difficulties. We know that from the 1898 Poincaré paper (Gray 1997, 27–39), where he identified in the classical three-body problem a behavior that today is identified as chaos. I mention this because I believe that what computer simulations can do in the future, and are partially already doing now, is filling up this knowledge gap where reasonable theories do not (yet) exist. I will come to this again later.

In addition there are many special physical theories, like solid-state physics, quantum optics, hadron physics, plasma physics, and others. The point is, that for all of these theories there are of course still open scientific questions, and there are always limits of applicability. But despite this situation, there is still no cry for new theories. What is often done successfully is to take a well-established theory and develop an extension into a larger domain of applicability.

My next statement refers to the structure of a physical theory (Ludwig 2012): **A (well-established) physical theory is a kind of functor from the set of physical phenomena to a set of mathematical objects.**

Thus a theory corresponds to an unambiguous assignment of physical phenomena to certain mathematical objects, that is, it is a kind of mapping that preserves the relations between the corresponding objects. This functor is verified by physical experiments. Preferably it will be invertible, because one should be able to make verifiable (falsifiable) predictions from derived mathematical theorems.

Phenomena	Represented by
A stone	Point in phase space (six-dimensional Euclidean space for the space and momentum coordinates)
Moves on trajectory	Solution of a set of differential equations
The stone as a system	A vector field on phase space
Initial conditions	Initial position and momentum (or velocity)
Parameters	Mass, etc.
Boundary conditions	Restriction for applicable forces, friction, etc.

[Fig. 1] Phenomena and their Representations

To make clearer what this means let us look at a well-known example in classical mechanics. To describe what happens if we throw a stone in a certain direction what a physicist will do first is to abstract from the stone and reduce it to a description of a mass point (see Fig. 1). This mass point is then represented as (mapped to) a mathematical point (a zero-dimensional object) in the so-called state space or phase space of the system. The observable trajectory of that stone will then be described as a solution of a set of corresponding differential equations.

The stone as a physical system (i.e., the stone together with all its possible trajectories resulting from all possible initial start points and initial velocities), is then described by a so-called vector field on state space. This will be a complete mathematical representation of all the motions this stone can realize. To obtain a specific trajectory, that is, a specific solution, one has to specify, besides the initial conditions, the relevant parameters of the system; for instance, the mass in this case. One also has to take relevant boundary conditions into account; for example, that the force one can apply is limited. Then one also has to specify those forces acting in addition to gravity on the system, such as friction. This is a satisfying classical characterization of a system like a stone. It is a heavily idealized mathematical description concerning measurable, physical quantities. It is not an attempt to describe the underlying real-world process that led to these measurements: this was stated by very many scientists, for instance by Feynman and Bohr.

If one accepts this definition of a physical theory then, of course, one must assert that quantum mechanics is a very well-established theory, and in fact it is—particularly as quantum field theory—the best verified physical theory we have so far. Why then should one ask for a new theory for this domain of atomic scale phenomena? There are at least two different arguments coming to my mind. One argument is based on the observation that quantum mechanics is a linear theory (linear in its state variables). Furthermore, following a more formal procedure to derive quantum mechanics from classical mechanics (Sniatycki 1980) one realizes that in principle one is able to quantize exactly only dynamically "trivial" systems like the harmonic oscillator (corresponding to a frictionless ideal pendulum). But the more interesting classical problems are of nonlinear and dissipative type, as I will discuss later. And one might question if there should be a more general "nonlinear quantum theory."

Another string of arguments stems from the observation that somehow one runs into difficulties if one wants to extend the application of quantum mechanical principles, which work so convincingly on the atomic and nuclear levels, into other domains like that of strong forces or gravitation. From a theoretician's point of view one would prefer to have a "theory of everything," based on universal principles and unifying the description of all fundamental forces and their phenomena.

One may augment these statements about physical theories by saying that these theories—as idealizations clearly formulated in mathematical terms—are as good as the perturbation theories belonging to them. This is of course due to the fact that the real-world processes are always "noisy" and have to be tamed by experimentalists in laboratory settings.

A third simple statement I want to make is the following: **Every physical theory is only as good as its underlying abstractions.**

I think this is an essential aspect and I want to mention it here because it tells you that we should be very open when we are looking for new theories, and especially for those in the context discussed in this workshop. This is because we make some fundamental assumptions about observed phenomena like interference. Do we have to deal with particles or waves? Or do we need new concepts for whatever it is between the source and the detector of an experiment? And perhaps one should remember that all the abstractions we are using in non-classical physics are still coming from the macroscopic world. So they are deduced from what our sensors receive from phenomena in the macroscopic world. From that it seems clear that abstractions so derived may not be optimal for processes acting in a different domain of phenomena.

To be a little bit clearer about what I mean by that, let me give a few examples.

As we have seen, objects like stones, cannon balls, bird feathers and things like that are in classical theories represented by mass points; that is, they are abstracted from all their properties like form, color, smell, roughness of the surface, and other properties that are thought to be irrelevant for the description of their movement in space.

Another essential concept is that of a free particle, meaning that there is no force acting on it. If one defines it, following in a way Aristotle in his *Physics*,[1] as an object that comes to rest at a finite time—which is what we will always observe—then the concept of a force like friction will not be developed. On the other hand, if, as with Newton (1999), a free particle is an object moving in a straight line with constant velocity then—by observing the orbit of the moon around Earth—one has to introduce a force, giving birth to the gravitational force. By the way: force is the most mystical concept in physics.

---

1   Compare for instance Rovelli, Carlo. 2015. "Aristotle's Physics: A Physicist's Look." *Journal of the American Philosophical Association*, 1(1): 23–40.

Another powerful abstraction is that of a vacuum. If one states—following Galileo (1953)—that every object near the earth falls with a constant acceleration, this again is not what one observes in reality: if you throw a marble or bird feather from the tower of Pisa, you will observe that they fall to earth differently.

Formulating a rule like Galileo did is making a very strong abstraction, which makes a comprehension of the observed processes only then accessible; in fact there is no physical vacuum in the real world.

Deriving such powerful abstractions from observed processes has always been—and always will be—the cornerstone for the development of new physical theories. Is it possible to derive such abstractions from computer simulations of physical systems?

Another problem that might be of relevance in the context of this workshop is declaring what a fundamental physical object is. For example: What is an elementary particle like the electron for which we observe the described scattering phenomena, and how can we simulate it?

There was (and still is) a long debate going on about how to answer this question, and if it is really necessary to assume elementary objects into which the world can be dissected and from which it can be synthesized again. As far as I know, already Heisenberg's paper of 1955 claimed that there are no real physical criteria to discern between an elementary object and a compound system (Heisenberg 1957, 269), i.e., a system that is built of many convenient parts. This difficulty when dealing with a concept of fundamental or elementary objects is due to the situation in elementary particle physics (i.e., strong forces physics), during the 1950s and beginning of the 1960s, where one identified around 130 elementary particles according to the then actual definitions. Of course everyone then asked the question: What is elementary about 130 particles? Naturally, there then were some quite different approaches that tried to rethink what should be postulated as being elementary, or which tried to abandon the concept of something being fundamental at all. One may mention the S-matrix theory and bootstrapping (Chew 1966) or von Weizsäcker's Ur-Theory (von Weizsäcker 1985), among many others. Those were very inspiring days for theoretical physicists, which came to a sudden end with the postulation of quarks as fundamental objects. And this end of the "particle zoo" demonstrates the power of a theory, because the demanded existence of (initially three) quarks (Gell-Mann 1964, 214–215) comes from pure mathematical beauty, namely symmetry, and there is no other reason. Strangely enough, the theory claims that quarks are unobservable as free particles.

Based on the underlying group theoretical methods one was able to set up a theory not only for hadron physics, but also for the domain of electro-magnetism and weak forces; a theory called the "standard model" today. This left us with the challenge of building up a unified theory of all forces (i.e., including gravitation)—a challenge that was not met until today.

Anyway, as was stated somewhere: "Without a guiding theory scientific explorations resemble endless forays in unknown territories. On the other hand, a theory allows us to identify fundamental characteristics, and avoid stumbling over fascinating idiosyncrasies and incidental features. It provides landmarks to orient ourselves in unknown grounds."

But enough about physical theories! What to say about computer simu-lations of physical phenomena and their relation to physical theories? I think it is remarkable to observe that at the same time that there was great confusion about what the fundamental physical objects should be, there was a growing awareness that the most interesting phenomena in the physical world result from nonlinear effects; that is, nonlinear systems are ubiquitous—and as the mathematician Stanislaw Ulam observed, to speak of "nonlinear science" is like "referring to the bulk of zoology as the study of non-elephant animals" (Campbell 1985, 374).

There was an upcoming feeling that new types of theories were needed to describe the diversity of these nonlinear phenomena. One may refer for instance to the work of Prigogine (Nicolis and Prigogine 1977) and Haken (1984). And new insights were driven in an accelerating sequence by the growing available computer power. There was the Lorenz equation (Lorenz 1963, 130–141), giving the first nonlinear model for weather dynamics. It was the first example of chaotic dynamics inherited by so many simple math-ematical equations, as was shown in the famous book of Mandelbrot (1983). There was also a formulation of global nonlinear dynamics by Hirsch and Smale (1974), applied to physics (Abraham and Marsden 1978), which was progressively noticed in the 1960s and 1970s. Finally it became clear that a desirable nonlinear theory has to describe the behavior of something like "complex adaptive systems" (Gell-Mann 1994, 17–45), a concept that is still under development. This can be marked by the foundation of the Santa Fe Institute in 1984. Now, concepts like nonlinearity, chaos, fractals, emergence, and complexity gathered more and more attention, and at the same time physics as a leading science was superseded by biology.

Already in 1953 it was (probably) Fermi who invented something like the concept of numerical experiments by proposing that instead of simply performing the standard calculation doing pencil and paper work, one could use a computer to test also physical hypotheses (Weissert 1997). At that time the Fermi–Pasta–Ulam group tried to understand the behavior of atoms in a crystal. To do simple things first, they reduced the problem to a one-dimensional problem considering a chain of mass points coupled by springs that obey Hooke's law; that is, they introduced a linear interaction. This linear problem is then something one can handle with classical theories. Needing a chain of masses of infinite length one will end up naturally with statistical physics. In this situation it was asked, what happens if one puts into these linear equations a very small nonlinear term. The well-known answer from statistical physics was: the energy of the system will finally be equally distributed over all the possible modes of the mass chain.

So, a simulation of the system with the equations augmented by a nonlinear term was run, and what was observed was very surprising: the energy does not drift towards the equipartition predicted by statistical physics, but periodically returns to the original mode. This was very difficult to understand and it was not predicted by any theory. In fact, this result led to a new field in physics centered on soliton theory.

What I think should be mentioned here is something quite characteristic for simulations of nonlinear systems: almost unexpectedly there do appear to be phenomena adhering to the simulated system that are unexpected and unexplainable, and they become manifest only by chance. In the Fermi–Pasta–Ulam case "the quasi-periodic behavior wasn't observed at first, because the computer was too slow to allow a simulation to run for long enough. But one day the computer wasn't stopped as intended, and the calculation was left running. The researchers found to their great surprise that nearly all of the energy returned to the initial mode, and the original state was almost perfectly recovered" (Dauxois 2008, 55–57).

The situation at that time was nicely described by Norman Zabusky, who said, "Now with the advent of large computers, sophisticated graphical algorithms and interactive terminals, we can undertake large-scale numerical simulations of systems and probe those regions of parameter space that are not easily accessible to the theorist/analyst or experimentalist" (cited by Weissert 1997). The Fermi–Pasta–Ulam simulations showed for the first time that computer simulations as a scientific tool can lead to phenomena inherited by physical systems, which are neither predicted by, nor expected from, the theories then at hand.

Nowadays computer simulations find widespread application in many different domains. For instance, they are used for predicting the behavior of physical systems, for proving the existence of hypothesized effects, for testing alternative approaches to a problem, or to explore the behavior of a model in new or larger parameter domains. And sometimes computer simulations also reveal unexpected phenomena, hidden in well-established theories. The best example is perhaps the visualization of chaotic behavior in a simple quadratic map, like the logistic map $f(x) = r \times (1-x)$ (Feigenbaum 1978), where r is the parameter determining the general behavior. This first and well-known example already points to the decisive role of the chosen visualization of computer simulation results.

For more clarification, let me finally unfold what I mean by a computer simulation: **A computer simulation realizes the behavior of a model system under certain boundary conditions for a given set of parameters.**

I want to point out that to have a convincing simulation you have to make sure that all three ingredients—the model, its parameters and the boundary conditions—are well defined. Thus, computer simulations in general follow a standard setup: first, there is a model (or a set of models) of the physical system under study. The model is given by a set of mathematical equations, usually based on an appropriate physical theory. In general this set of equations will have a finite set of parameters for which the behavior of the system should be studied. The specification of the parameter domain is essential for conditioning the applicability of the results derived from the simulation. In addition, appropriate boundary conditions determining the "environment" and the initial conditions for starting a process have to be fixed.

It should be clear that every model picks up only certain aspects of a phenomenon and neglects others that are considered marginal with respect to the particular investigation. But the quality of the utilized models depends essentially on an appropriate mathematical formulation, eventually added by interesting terms, like in the Fermi–Pasta–Ulam case, or just by some interesting mathematically motivated equations. Models are of course always reasonable reductions, abstractions, approximations or analogs of the real physical systems they mimic. In addition, one often has to deal with a large set of parameters for which the behavior has to be tested, and that is what larger computer power is usually needed for.

For many interesting problems of today it is a quite difficult task to set up reliable models and to identify crucial parameter domains, because the intrinsic complexity of the investigated systems and their environments is still increasing due to the involved stochastic properties and nonlinearities. Furthermore, these systems are often composed of many subsystems, so questions like that of system-level organization, development, interdependence, and interactions of subsystems have to be considered carefully, as well as the interaction of the compound system with its often challenging environment. And the parameter sets then have to be thoughtfully adjusted to the posed problem. One therefore often has to go through a cyclic procedure: modeling, simulating, analyzing the results, adaptation of model and parameters, simulating again, and so on.

One way to categorize the many variants of practicing computer simulations is to follow John Holland (2012) by discerning data-driven models, existence-proof models, and exploratory models. These are outlined below.

The *data-driven models* are the common ones used to establish good predictions or a better understanding of processes of interest like climate, weather, traffic, car crashes, bomb explosions, and so on. For these simulations one usually has a given set of mathematical equations, which are derived from an established theory, and a well-defined set of parameters. A comparison of the simulation's results with observed data should then lead to a more precise simulation by adjusting relevant terms in the mathematical equations and tuning the respective parameters. These data-driven simulations mostly give answers of the causal if/then type: if the following initial conditions are satisfied then one will observe the following behavior.

Existence-proof models are used to prove the hypothetical existence of phenomena in certain not yet observed or explored parameter domains and initial conditions. A typical example for this category of computer simulations is von Neumann's hypothesis (von Neumann and Burks 1966, 3–14) that self-reproducing machines do exist. The positive answer to this question we nowadays enjoy as the game of life. Another of the many examples, which was also reported by newspapers, was that the existence of monster waves—which have long been around as a vivid fantasy of sailors—has now been proved by computer simulations. Physicists showed that a combination of linear and nonlinear terms in corresponding wave equations could lead to the spontaneous appearance of monster waves, which are not announced in advance by the slow buildup of a superposition of normal waves (Adcock, Taylor, and Draper 2015).

The goal of *exploratory models* is oriented towards answering questions concerning processes that correspond to rather abstract models of systems or to problems for which a theory or a reasonable mathematization is not (yet) available. They are often purely based on computer programs representing for instance something like *Gedanken* experiments. Often they are driven by the goal of realizing a certain fictional system or optimizing a desired procedure, but neither a mathematical method nor a reasonable theory is known for doing so. Exploratory computer-based models have much in common with the traditional thought experiments of physics. One selects some interesting mechanisms and then explores the consequences that occur when these mechanisms interact in some carefully contrived setting. These experimental settings are often not achievable in a laboratory; hence, the "laboratory" resides in the head.

To give again an example reported in the newspapers: artificial diamonds were realized in a microwave reactor. To achieve this result a group of scientists at the Diamond Foundry (diamondfoundry.com) company first simulated tens of thousands of different mixtures of ingredients in different reactor shapes to finally obtain in reality an extremely hot plasma under very high pressure at a certain localization. Other examples can be taken from synthetic biology. Here one of the goals is for instance to build regulatory circuits of proteins that are able to control cell behavior. With respect to basic research the aim is to construct—among others—a living artificial biological cell. In the first attempts computer simulations were used to identify a kind of minimal genome that allows for a living cell. Then this genome was chemically synthesized and injected into a bacterium (Hutchison et al. 2016) demonstrating that it is sufficient to realize a living cell. Without the tremendous computer power available it is impossible to find the necessary protein reactions.

For these exploratory simulations therefore (complete) knowledge about a system is not applied but generated. In fact, a theory-driven comprehension of observable real processes is replaced by an experience with possible structures and processes, which is based on specific simulations using large computer capacities. This kind of experience with the simulation of exploratory model systems, which may have no counterparts in the physical world, will not necessarily lead to new theories. But it leads to very many desired applications following the slogan, *I do not understand how it works, but I know how to do it*. With respect to the natural sciences, complex computer simulations often replace *tinkering in the lab* with *modeling in the computer*, and referring to scientific explorations without a theory one may state that *understanding is replaced by engineering techniques*.

After having described what I understand by a physical theory and having surveyed different types of computer simulations, I will shortly come back to event-based simulations.

The goal of these simulations was to demonstrate that for certain scattering experiments the results predicted by quantum theory are reproducible by assuming purely classical arguments. This is done by showing that the statistical distributions of quantum theory can be reproduced "by modeling physical phenomena as a chronological sequence of events whereby events can be actions of an experimenter, particle emissions by a source, signal generations by a detector, interactions of a particle with a material" (Michielsen and De Raedt 2014, 2).

Now, what is the setup of these simulations? To begin with we have three different models: one for the source, one for the detector, and one for what is in *between*. All these models are claimed to be derived from properties ascribed to objects of classical physics. All of these models have several parameters that can be tuned in such a way as to reproduce the interference pattern observed in laboratory experiments (ibid.).

According to the classifications given above, to which categories can we assign event-based simulations? Of course they do not use data-driven models. But they have aspects of existence-proof simulations in so far as they try models of classical systems able to reproduce the observed interference patterns. Although they are exploring the effects of different models and parameters concerning the involved subsystems (source, detectors, and the "between"), they are not exploratory computer simulations because the behavior of the compound system to be reproduced is given beforehand by the laboratory experiments.

What hampers event-based simulations—as they stand now—to give guidance for the development of a new physical theory is then obvious. It is of course the role of the models and parameters in this context. Replacing an electron with a "messenger" in a scattering is for the moment only an exchange of the naming for what is "between" the source and the detector. But the quantum mechanical electron has many additional properties, like quantum numbers identifying it as a lepton, and therefore makes possible the prediction of the outcomes of many other experimental settings. For every new type of experimental setup the "messenger" has to be modeled anew, together with different models for the source and especially for the detectors. Furthermore, all these models have many tunable parameters, which allow adapting simulation results to those obtained from the physical experiments performed in a laboratory. Another question is if event-based simulations can make observable predictions of new phenomena—as any convincing theory is expected to provide.

To summarize: my impression is that at the moment the event-based simulation approach merely replaces for a certain set of physical experiments the "mysterious" quantum theoretical interpretations with a no less "mysterious" signal messenger or "mailman." If in the future there will be an accumulated experience with event-based simulations giving a more consistent view of how to describe microscopic, atomic, or even subatomic phenomena, my view may be changed. Knowing about the impact of computer simulations on generating new concepts and "world views" one may still hope to excavate certain properties of the physical world, or powerful abstractions of those, which then can inspire or trigger a new type of physical theory having again a formal mathematical description.

References

Abraham, Ralph, and Jerrold E. Marsden. 1978. *Foundations of Mechanics*. Reading, MA: Benjamin/Cummings Publishing Company.

Adcock, Thomas AA, Paul H. Taylor, and Scott Draper. 2015. "Nonlinear dynamics of wavegroups in random seas: unexpected walls of water in the open ocean." *Proceedings of the Royal Society A*, 471 (2184).

Campbell, David K. Jim Crutchfield, Doyne Farmer, and Erica Jen. 1985. "Experimental Mathematics: The Role of Computation in Nonlinear Science", *Communications of the ACM* 28 (4): 374–384.

Chew, Geoffrey F. 1966. *The Analytic S Matrix: a Basis for Nuclear Democracy*. New York: WA Benjamin.

Dauxois, Thierry. 2008. "Fermi, Pasta, Ulam, and a mysterious lady." *Physics Today* 61 (1): 55–57.

Feigenbaum, Mitchell J. 1978. "Quantitative Universality for a Class of Nonlinear Transformation." J. Stat. Phys. 19 (1): 25–52.

Feynman, Richard. 1989. *The Feynman Lectures on Physics: Commemorative Issue, Vol. 3 Quantum Mechanics 1-1*. Boston: Addison Wesley.

Galilei, Galileo. 1953. *Dialogue Concerning the Two Chief World Systems*. Translated by Stillman Drake. Los Angeles: University of California Press.

Gray, Jeremy. 1997. "Poincaré in the archives-two examples." *Philosophia Scientiae* 2 (3): 27–39.

Gell-Mann, Murray. 1964. "A Schematic Model of Baryons and Mesons." *Physics Letters* 8: 214–215.

Gell-Mann, Murray. 1994. *Complex Adaptive Systems*. Boston: Addison-Wesley.

Haken, Hermann. 1984. *The Science of Structure: Synergetics*. New York: Van Nostrand Reinhold Company.

Heisenberg, Werner. 1957. "Quantum theory of fields and elementary particles." *Reviews of Modern Physics* 29 (3).

Hirsch, Morris, and Stephen Smale. 1974. *Differential Equations, Dynamical Systems, and Linear Algebra*. New York: Academic Press.

Holland, John H. 2012. *Signals and Boundaries: Building Blocks for Complex Adaptive Aystems*. Cambridge, MA: MIT Press.

Hutchison, Clyde A. III, Ray-Yuan Chuang, Vladimir N. Noskov, Nacyra Assad-Garcia, Thomas J. Deerinck, Mark H. Ellisman, John Gill, Krishna Kannan, Bogumil J. Karas, Li Ma, James F. Pelletier, Zi-Qing Qi, R. Alexander Richter, Elizabeth A. Strychalski, Lijie Sun, Yo Suzuki, Billyana Tsvetanova, Kim S. Wise, Hamilton O. Smith, John I. Glass, Chuck Merryman, Daniel G. Gibson, and J. Craig Venter. 2016. "Design and synthesis of a minimal bacterial genome." *Science* 351 (6280): aad6253.

Lorenz, Edward N. 1963. "Deterministic nonperiodic flow." *Journal of the Atmospheric Sciences* 20 (2): 130–141.

Ludwig, Günther. 2012. *Foundations of Quantum Mechanics I*. Berlin: Springer Science & Business Media.

Mandelbrot, Benoît B. 1983. *The Fractal Geometry of Nature*. San Francisco: W.H. Freeman.

Michielsen, Kristel, and Hans De Raedt. 2014. "Event-based simulation of quantum physics experiments." *International Journal of Modern Physics* C 25 (08): 1430003.

Newton, Isaac. 1999. *The Principia: Mathematical Principles of Natural Philosophy*. Berkeley, CA: University of California Press.

Nicolis, G., and I. Prigogine. 1977. *Self-Organization in Nonequilibrium Systems: From Dissipative Structures to Order Through Fluctuations*. New York: Wiley

Sniatycki, Jedrzej. 1980. *Geometric Quantization and Quantum Mechanics*. New York, Berlin: Springer Verlag.

von Neumann, John, and Arthur W. Burks. 1966. "Theory of self-reproducing automata." *IEEE Transactions on Neural Networks* 5 (1): 3–14.

von Weizsäcker, Carl Friedrich. 1985. *Der Aufbau der Physik*. Munich: Hanser.

Weissert, Thomas P. 1997. *The Genesis of Simulation in Dynamics*. Berlin: Springer Verlag.

Discussion with Frank Pasemann

Stefan Zieme: I'd like to go back to the very beginning, to the first statement you made. You said every physical theory describes a well-defined area of phenomena. My question would be what to your belief is a phenomenon, and even further can there be a phenomenon without a theory?

Frank Pasemann: I used it here in the naïve sense, referring to objects, processes or facts observed in the physical world by our senses. Talking about physics I naturally understand our measuring apparatuses to be an extension of our human senses. What was called an "event" by Kristel [Michielsen] and Hans [De Raedt] is related to that. Can there be a phenomenon without a theory? To a certain extent this question refers to a kind of chicken-and-egg problem. I would say in general you do not need a theory to observe something I called a phenomenon. On the other hand a theory sometimes claims that something—an effect, a process—should be observable and it gives a name for it. For what we were discussing here I would call the observable "interference pattern" predicted by quantum theory a phenomenon, but not the electrons, quantum probability waves, or any kind of descriptive "messenger." These are wordings used in the specific context of theories or simulations.

Hans-Jörg Rheinberger: If you are coming from biology and not from physics, this is I would say an everyday situation, that you can have and even stabilize and reproduce phenomena without having a theory in the background. You can do genetics – classical genetics – in a quantitative manner without having to know anything about the material constitution of the hereditary units. I think that's very common in the life sciences.

FP: I believe that the development of the biological sciences had a great influence on the way we are reflecting natural processes today because, compared to the standard physical systems, biology has to deal with much more complex and differentiated structures. Perhaps biologists are much closer to thinking in terms of dynamics, of "noisiness," of networks and coherent subsystems. That is perhaps the point where the "New Science" is developing.

Eric Winsberg: I think that's also the case in physics. I think the expressions you used, stable and reproducible, those are I think what are characteristic of phenomena. It's not just something that you see happen in the world, but it's something that can be reproduced consistently and you get the same kind of data pattern from a variety of different apparatus and such. Which may or may not fall under a theory—it's when you have stable and reproducible phenomena that don't fall under a theory that you think well, gee, maybe I need new theory.

SZ: Let me give an example: I thought about what is the phenomenon, what stage to understand it. Looking at the sky every night, you can produce data about where the planets go. You can look at the data, you can have a pattern of recognition, you can say they move in an ellipsis. It's the phenomenon, the data or the ellipsis. Because ellipsis is not a phenomenon. Firstly it's wrong, they don't move in an ellipsis. They can only do so if you choose a theory. My question was where would you put the phenomena? At which stage? I think you are at the second stage.

FP: And let me make a remark also about stability. The nice thing about our everyday world is that it is almost stable; there is no stability in an absolute sense. Of course we would not exist if atoms and the things composed of them were not stable on a certain time scale. But stability is still a concept to think about, due to the fact that often only a configuration of elements is relatively stable, not their parts. Think about a dynamic equilibrium. Due to the relative stability of the macroscopic physical world we were able to develop first of all classical mechanics, giving a deeper understanding of our everyday world. But as we see nowadays that is not the whole story.

For me the phenomena are the moving planets in the sky. Measuring their advancing positions will result in a set of data. Now, an ellipsis for me is primarily a mathematical object. It may be used to fit the data of the planets' positions. But the ellipsis may also be a solution curve of some differential equations, provided by a physical theory, representing the idealized movements of celestial bodies.

SZ: Do you think it is necessary to have a theory as you have described it for the development of physical science?

FP: No, not at all. I therefore referred to a "well-established" theory like classical mechanics or quantum mechanics. If you are active in a new field or stumble over some new phenomena it may be better to forget about such a definite theory. In these situations usually one will talk about things in terms of working definitions; for instance, one uses terms like roughness, fractality, chaos, nonlinearity or complexity to point to repeating patterns of observations and properties. Most of the time a mathematical theory comes after certain relations between phenomena are aggregated and consolidated. So a mathematical theory can refer to a deeper understanding of what determines these relations.

MW: What if you would introduce the media of science into your world view? It all looks so ideal once again. It has no materiality, theory building is coming and going. I do not understand yet how theories could come and go? What do you think about introducing the concept of media on which sciences rely? That would change this ideal situation.

FP: Yes, theories are coming and going, that is a "natural process." How did Newton come up with his theory, and where is his theory going? It simply was absorbed in another, more comprehensive theory. Other theories have to go because new ones generate better data, produce more interesting, verifiable predictions, and the like.

As I said, as mathematical theories they are idealizations. Take classical electrodynamics: you can write it down in two equations with only a few symbols. It is a "medium" to understand all the electromagnetic phenomena of the everyday world. It has an epistemological function, and as such it depends on the actual "world view"—that's what I referred to as abstractions. I suppose that theories, as media of science, are forms of organizing our scientific experience of the physical world. Perhaps mathematical theories are a sort of "hot media" in the sense of McLuhan, and what one is using a theory for depends very much on the community that is trying to apply it. With the widespread use of computer simulations, as a kind of "cool" medium perhaps even the "hotness" of theories will change.

Moreover, if we call the mathematical theories "hot" theories, it's the "cool" theories that have a substantial impact on the developing sciences. Think about "chaos theory," which is still based on different "working definitions" but has influenced many, and not only scientific, fields of interest.

On the other hand, take a beautiful mathematical theory like string theory: because the community is able or willing to think about operations in 11 or 13 dimensions, its influence on our "world view," our technological or social development (at the moment), is quite negligible. It seemingly does not have the aura of a popular medium.

But to answer your question: I do not know if using the notion of media of sciences for physical theories will change the way we will try to understand physical phenomena. Anyway, to say it in today's parlance: it is cool to have a theory.

Arianna Borrelli: You mentioned that computer simulation could contribute, for example in this case of complex systems, where you don't really have any mathematical tools, but before, earlier in your talk you mentioned the interesting questions open at the theoretical level. For example unification—you spoke about unification of forces. I was wondering, don't you think, for example, simulations could contribute to that? Of course unification between say electromagnetism and gravity is what everybody is working on—I mean not everybody, but many. Of course there could be possibility of trying to unify quantum mechanics and quantum field theory, which are not unified. I don't know if anyone is working on that. I was wondering, I ask you because this is something I often wonder about because there's a lot of talk about unification at this high level and there is so little unification at the level where one could also work. So I was just wondering, since we have talked before about this problem of one particle and of many particles. Could that be a possibly interesting or promising direction?

FP: Yes, of course. The point is that in the "old" days you could sit down, have some nice idea, write some equations on paper, and then calculate the possible effects. Nowadays we are confronted with more sophisticated problems. To get some reasonable results from your possibly good ideas it will take substantial computer power, a group to work on them, and not least, quite a bit of money. With respect to unification I can for instance imagine using simulations to study physics in higher dimensions, without relying on mathematical devices like group theory. If in these simulations your apple still falls down to earth and, in addition, all the other observed (and possibly not yet observed) processes are presented, then perhaps you have understood something essential—without having (yet) a theory.

6

Quantum Theory: A Media-Archaeological Perspective

Arianna Borrelli

Introduction: Computer Simulations as a Complement to Quantum Theory?

In this paper I will provide some historical perspectives on the question at the core of this workshop, namely the many ways in which computer simulations may be contributing to reshape science in general and quantum physics in particular. More specifically, I would like to focus on the issue of whether computer simulations may be regarded as offering an alternative, or perhaps a complementary, version of quantum theory. I will not be looking at the way in which computer simulations are used in quantum physics today, since this task has been outstandingly fulfilled by other contributions to this workshop. Instead, I will present a few episodes from the history of quantum theory in such a way as to make it plausible that simulations might indeed provide the next phase of historical development.

In what sense can computer simulations be regarded as "theories," though? How can a computer simulation be on a par with the Schrödinger equation of quantum mechanics? To answer this question I will start by discussing (and criticizing) the rather naïve, but very widespread ideal of "theory" that dominates much of today's fundamental physical research, and of which quantum mechanics constitutes a paradigmatic example.

There is little doubt that quantum mechanics is seen today as an epistemically privileged physical-mathematical construct, and this status is hardly surprising, because quantum mechanics provides the basis for a large number of experimentally successful quantitative predictions. However, the predictive efficacy is by far not the only factor supporting the authority of quantum mechanics. Of paramount importance is the fact that it conforms to an ideal of theory that emerged in the course of the nineteenth century and still largely dominates physical research today: a "theory" as a coherent, rigorous mathematical construct expressed in symbolic formulas from which testable numerical predictions can (at least in principle) be derived. Such a construct may then be coupled to a physical interpretation expressed in verbal terms, to deliver not only predictions, but also explanations of phenomena. As I have discussed at length in other publications (Borrelli 2012; 2015a; 2015b), this image of a physical-mathematical construct both numerically predicting and verbally explaining phenomena is a fundamental template of authority in the physical sciences (and often also beyond them), despite the fact that not even long-established "theories" such as classical mechanics or electromagnetism actually conform to it.

Few, if any, mathematical theories can remain coherent and rigorous if they also have to provide procedures for actually computing predictions. Even in those very rare cases in which an equation like Schrödinger's can be solved exactly, applying the solution to a real-world case always requires adjusting it in some way that will make it not any more coherent with the original equation. In quantum mechanics the connection of Schrödinger's equation with phenomena is particularly problematic, because in the standard Copenhagen interpretation the measurement process is assumed to irreversibly change the state of the quantum system. During a measurement, in the standard interpretation, a so-called reduction of the wave function occurs: the wave function associated with the quantum state immediately before the measurement is instantaneously replaced by a different one that reflects the outcome of the measurement.[1] In other words, there is no coherent mathematical structure capable of modeling the process of measurement in a quantum system.

---

1   On the Copenhagen interpretation of quantum mechanics, the measurement problem and the alternative interpretations proposed since the 1950s (see Faye 2014). It is not my intention to discuss here interpretative issues of quantum mechanics, since no satisfactory solution for the measurement problem has been found so far, and the Copenhagen interpretation remains the dominating one, at least among practicing physicists.

In general, the image of a theory as a rigorous and coherent mathematical construct from which numerical predictions can be derived has little or no correspondence in actual research. Yet this image still dominates science and endows constructs like the Schrödinger equation with a special authority. A key feature of this special status is that, both in today's scientific culture and in the popular imagination, symbolic formulas are usually regarded as mere vehicles to convey abstract, disembodied conceptual structures whose features are fully independent from the form in which they are expressed.

In contrast to this view of theoretical knowledge, I believe that theories are "abstract" only in the sense of being far removed from everyday experience, not in the sense of being "disembodied." Science is first and foremost a collective enterprise, and so no theory can exist that is not expressed, communicated, and appropriated by means of some aesthetically perceivable form, such as symbols, words, diagrams, three-dimensional models—and perhaps also computer simulations. Mathematical symbols, for example, are obviously visual and, for those who are familiar with the rules for manipulating them, they also possess a haptic component (Borrelli 2010; Krämer et al. 2012; Velminski and Werner 2010). This material and performative dimension of theories does not allow a sharp separation of form and content and is an essential factor shaping their employment in research practices. To put it in other terms, I would like to claim that the dynamics of medium and message apply also to physical theories.

Therefore I will now discuss some episodes from the history of quantum theory by highlighting the role of the material, performative dimension. I will show how, in the early days of quantum theory, the range of forms mediating theories was much broader than one might expect. I will argue that, if we set aside the ideal of theory as a disembodied construct necessarily manifesting itself only in rigorous mathematical formulas, there is little difficulty in considering computer simulations as a medium of quantum theory on a par with the many symbolic and diagrammatic constructs that were developed in the pioneering years of the discipline.

Spectroscopy between Arithmetics and Geometry

I begin my overview by considering what is today referred to as "classical physics", that is, the many theories developed or refined over the course of the nineteenth century, such as mechanics, electromagnetism, acoustics or hydrodynamics. In that context, there was one medium of theory enjoying a very privileged status: differential equations and the functions solving them. Differential equations worked very well in delivering numerical predictions for a wide range of phenomena, but some areas appeared problematic. The experimental field that most decisively contributed to the rise of quantum theory was the study of light and its properties, and more precisely the phenomena of spectral lines and black-body radiation. It was in those contexts that refined differential equations came to be replaced by very simple arithmetic formulas as the most effective medium to theoretically capture observation.

Already in the early modern period it had been accepted that white light resulted from a superposition of colored rays, and when in the nineteenth century the wave theory of light became established, each colored ray that could not be further decomposed came to be associated with a wave of specific length and frequency. Around 1850 physicists noticed that the light produced by igniting different chemical elements was made out of different, discrete sets of colors (i.e., wavelengths).[2] By the late nineteenth century physicists had developed a new research object: "line spectra," that is, the sets of lines produced by decomposing the light emitted by various substances.

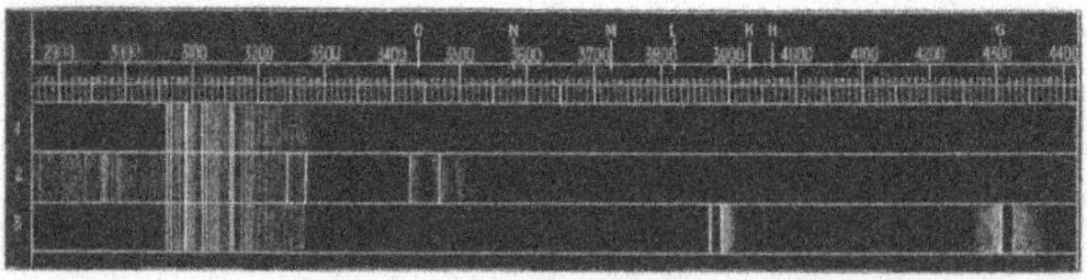

[Fig. 1] Line spectrum of hydrogen (Source: Huggins 1880, 577).

Line spectra such as the one of hydrogen shown in Fig. 1 clearly displayed a discontinuous character, with each element emitting light only of specific, discrete wavelengths, whose numerical values could be estimated by measuring the distance between the lines in the spectrum. The discontinuity of spectra was problematic because if microphysics was ruled by differential equations having smooth, continuous solutions, then the light emitted should have formed a continuous spectrum—not a discrete one.

Researchers at the time made various proposals for how to connect the experimental results with available theory. One approach often employed was to make an analogy between light spectra and acoustic vibrations,

2   The following overview of the development of spectroscopy and of spectral formula is based on Hentschel (2002). For the role of spectroscopy in the development of quantum theory see Jammer (1966).

which had been successfully represented in mathematical form through the so-called harmonics (i.e., Fourier series of sine and cosine functions). However, such approaches were not very fruitful, and the breakthrough occurred only with the proposal of Johann Jakob Balmer (1825–1898), who was not a physicist, but a mathematician and an architect, and in particular an expert in the field of architectural perspective drawing. Never having worked on spectroscopy before, Balmer in 1885 published a short paper in which he proposed that the wavelengths of the hydrogen spectral lines would conform to the very simple formula:

$$H(m, n) = h \frac{m^2}{m^2 + n^2}$$

with H the value of a given wavelength, (m, n) two integer numbers and h = 3,645 a constant computed on the basis of measurement (Balmer 1885, 81, 83). For m = 3, 4 and n = 2 Balmer's formula fit very well the measurements available, and in the following years it turned out that also for higher values of m and n the formula matched the wavelengths of newly observed hydrogen lines.

How did Balmer, a mathematician and architect who had never shown an interest in physics, arrive at his formula? We have no direct sources on this issue, but historian and philosopher of science Klaus Hentschel has offered a very plausible answer based on an analysis of Balmer's work and of archival material (Hentschel (2002, 295–301, 442–448; Hentschel 2008). In his 1885 paper Balmer did not explain how he had arrived at his formula, but some years later, in 1897, he again wrote about spectroscopy and showed how an improved expression could be derived based on a geometrical construction similar to those employed in architectural perspective drawing, in which Balmer was an expert (Balmer 1897). In his 1897 paper Balmer explained that the hydrogen wavelengths could be constructed geometrically as shown in the right half of Fig. 2.

First one should draw a circle whose diameter AO represents the minimum wavelength of hydrogen. Then the points 1, 2, 3... are drawn along the X-axis at equal distance from each other. By drawing the tangents to the circle passing from points 3, 4, ... and looking where they intersect the vertical axis, one obtains the wavelengths of the hydrogen spectrum as the distances between point O and the intersection points. This construction is the same as that employed to derive the perspective shortening of a circular column as seen by an observer walking along the X-axis and pausing to look at the column at points 3, 4 ...

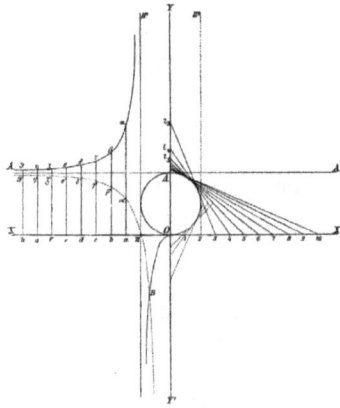

[Fig. 2] Geometrical derivation of spectroscopic formula (Source: Balmer 1897, plate VIII).

Hentschel argues that this geometrical derivation was similar to the way in which Balmer came to his formula in the first place: his experience with perspective drawing led him to visually perceive the spectral lines in terms of a familiar construction for the shortening of a fluted column. It is not possible for me to present here Hentschel's detailed argument, but an important point he makes is that while physicists at the time focused on an analogy between light and sound that was expressed in terms of frequencies and mathematical functions (harmonics), Balmer worked visually and geometrically, and so could open up new paths of reflection. Here we see an example of how the employment of different media to express the "same" knowledge could lead research in diverging directions. For us today Balmer's symbolic formula represents a physically significant result, which prompted the development of quantum theory, while his geo-metrical reasoning appears to be purely contingent. Yet Balmer saw geo-metrical methods as a significant guideline in research and, after describing the geometrical construction in Fig. 2, he stated:

> This construction may possibly be useful in throwing a new light on the mysterious phenomena of spectral lines, and in leading to the right way of finding the real closed formula for spectral wavelengths, in case it has not already been found in the formula of Rydberg. (Balmer 1897, 209)

Balmer's rule for deriving hydrogen spectral wavelengths could be
expressed both in arithmetical and geometrical terms, but the choice of
medium had epistemic implications. Balmer's contemporaries, perhaps
unsurprisingly, chose the arithmetic formulation, and today the idea of
using geometrical construction for theoretical guidelines may appear
very far-fetched. Yet it was probably geometrical reasoning that produced
Balmer's formula in the first place and, as we will presently see, theorists
later developing quantum theory did not shy away from very far-fetched
constructions expressed in symbolic notation.

By the early twentieth century Balmer's formula had been developed
into more general expressions for spectral series, according to which all
frequencies of light emitted by atoms could be expressed arithmetically as
the difference between two terms, each depending on a positive integer
(m, n), on the universal "Rydberg constant" R, and on a number of other
constants (s, p, d…) depending on the kind of atom.[3] The formula looked
like this:

$$v(m, n) = \frac{R}{(n + s)^2} - \frac{R}{(m + p)^2}$$

Such simple formulas could fit practically all the results of atomic spectroscopy, a rapidly expanding experimental field at the time. By finding
the values of the constants s, p etc. on the basis of the first few lines in a
series, predictions for lines with higher m, n could be obtained, and they
often turned out to be correct. The fact that the formulas were based on
integer numbers seemed at first surprising, and some authors at the time
tried to find a differential equation from which such formulas could be
derived, but in this early phase the search was to no avail (Hentschel 2012).
For more than a decade, the formulas for line spectra resisted all attempts
to embed them in an overarching physical-mathematical framework, or at
least provide them with a verbal interpretation with explanatory character.
The formulas remained what I would like to characterize as "mathematical
fragments," that is, physical-mathematical expressions which, although
complete in themselves, stood in isolation from the theoretical landscape
of their time. Theorists used them as starting points to try and construct
broader theoretical frameworks, treating them as though they might be
traces, "fragments" of a (hypothetical) overarching theory that had yet to
be formulated.

---

3   The information contained in the following overview on the development of
     quantum mechanics can be found for example in Jammer (1966). On the role of series
     formulas in the development of quantum theory see also Borrelli (2009; 2010).

In the early twentieth century spectral series were not the only "mathematical fragments" involving natural numbers that played a role in microphysics: there was also Planck's formula for black-body radiation. Like Balmer's formula, Planck's expression had been derived bottom-up by matching experimental results in a situation where all top-down derivations from electromagnetic theory had failed to provide empirically plausible predictions.[4] Planck's formula could be seen as implying that the energy exchange between matter and electromagnetic radiation could only take place in finite quantities, and that the minimum amount ("quantum") of energy exchanged by matter with light of frequency v was hv, where h was Planck's constant.

Bohr's Atom and the Old Quantum Theory as Multimedial Constructs

By the early twentieth century simple arithmetic formulas involving positive integer numbers had taken center stage in the search for a theory of "quantum" physics, and in 1913 the Danish theorist Niels Bohr (1885–1962) combined them with elements from classical physics and verbally formulated physical assumptions to produce "Bohr's atom," a very innovative theoretical construct.[5]

First of all Bohr assumed that the hydrogen atom could be regarded as a small solar system governed by a classical differential equation defining its possible orbits. Then he introduced a novel physical principle expressed verbally: only those orbits having certain particular values of the energy were actually realized, because only in them would the atom not radiate and would thus remained stable.[6] These stable orbits were called "stationary states" and, according to Bohr, radiation only occurred when the atom "jumped" from one stationary state to another. The energy E lost (or gained) by the atom corresponded to the creation (or annihilation) of light of frequency v such that E = hv, as required by Planck's formula. Each of the stationary energy levels was linked to an integer number, chosen so as to exactly match one of the two terms in the hydrogen series formula.

---

4   The history of the emergence and transformation of Planck's black-body formula has been studied in much detail by many historians and cannot be discussed here. A recent overview with further references is Badino (2015).

5   For a recent, exhaustive treatment of Bohr's atomic model and its development see Kragh (2012).

6   The stability of matter was a problem for the solar system atom in classical physics, since in classical electromagnetism a moving electron would radiate, lose energy, and eventually fall into the nucleus.

Since all spectral series formulas were differences between two similar terms, they could all be interpreted as expressing the difference between the initial and final energy of an atom. Clearly, the predictive value of Bohr's atom was identical to that of the spectral formulas on which it was based, so no new knowledge was actually obtained. However, now the "mathematical fragments" were connected to a more complex construct that involved both classical orbits and novel notions like "stationary states" and "quantum jumps"—a construct that is regarded as the first quantum theory, combining functions, arithmetic formulas, and verbal statements in what may be characterized as a multimedial whole. The fact that verbal statements played such a crucial role in Bohr's atom was typical of his work, and it is no accident that he is often highlighted as one of the most philosophical scientists of his time. Despite its hybrid, innovative character Bohr's atom was very positively received, and soon became the core of what is today known as the "old" quantum theory, which was developed between 1913 and 1925 by Bohr himself, and by many other authors.[7]

In the "old quantum theory" each possible stationary state of an atom was associated with a set of integer (or semi-integer) numbers derived by performing an increasing number of spectroscopic measurements, and then fitting these empirical results with spectral formulas containing the quantum numbers of the various stationary states. Although these sets of "quantum numbers" may appear to be nothing but a group of natural numbers, they actually constituted a new form of theoretical representation—a new medium of physical theory that was necessary to represent and manipulate the new notion of "stationary state." In principle, each stationary state was also associated with a classical orbit but, as the formal intricacy of the theory increased, quantum numbers became more and more the primary means to aesthetically represent and manipulate the innovative, and in many ways obscure, notion of stationary state introduced by Bohr.

Physical Quantities as Infinite Matrices

By 1925 quantum theory had proved to be capable of subsuming a large number of new experimental results in spectroscopy, but it still remained an extremely fragmentary construct that physicists kept on modifying and enlarging to accommodate new spectroscopic evidence. Scientists involved in this task usually justified their modus operandi by invoking Bohr's

---

7   For details of these developments see for example Kragh (2012), Jammer (1966), or Borrelli (2009).

"correspondence principle," a very flexible—not to say vague—heuristic tool to formally derive quantum relationships from classical ones. In 1925 the young physicist Werner Heisenberg (1901–1976) made a proposal for a new way of reframing and unifying the results obtained up to then, and further developed his suggestion together with Max Born (1882–1970) and Pascual Jordan (1902–1980).[8] The result of this process was "matrix mechanics," a theoretical construct perhaps even more innovative than Bohr's atom. Matrix mechanics was a theory expressed in part in verbal terms and in part through symbolic expressions, which although at first sight appeared to be mathematical structures in fact did not correspond with any rigorous, coherent objects of the mathematics of their time.

Matrix mechanics emerged quite rapidly over the course of a few months during 1925, but the process of its construction was extremely complex, and I will not attempt to summarize it. I will instead offer a brief overview of the new theory, arguing that it represented not only a fundamental step from a physical point of view, but also a further radical transformation of the way in which "quantum theories" were aesthetically made available to fellow scientists.

Just as was the case for Bohr's atom, matrix mechanics did not bring with it new testable predictions, but rather offered a different, more unitary set of rules for obtaining already known results. Matrix mechanics took over the key new elements from the old quantum theory: the idea of stationary states associated with sets of quantum numbers and that of quantum jumps from one state to another. Classical orbits were left out: Heisenberg explained that physics should only deal with "observables," and in atoms the only observable quantities are the frequencies and intensities of spectral lines, which are not linked to a single electron orbit but to the transition between the two of them. The exact position and velocity of an electron orbiting around the nucleus, on the other hand, are not observable and so should have no place in quantum theory. Heisenberg's key original idea was that quantum-physical quantities should not be theoretically conceived and represented as having at each instant a single numerical value, as was the case in classical physics, but rather thought of as always related to an infinite set of values. Accordingly, each physical quantity was associated with a set of infinitely many values, which were ordered into a two-dimensional matrix having infinitely many rows and columns. In the case of the hydrogen atom each row and each column was labeled by the quantum numbers of one hydrogen stationary state, as is seen in the formula below,

---

8   For an overview on the emergence of matrix mechanics see Jammer (1966, 196–220).

where "n" and "m" stand for one or more quantum numbers describing a stationary state.

$$\begin{bmatrix} M_{1,1} & M_{1,2} & \cdots & M_{1,m} & \cdots \\ \cdots & \cdots & \cdots & \cdots & \cdots \\ M_{n,1} & \cdots & \cdots & M_{n,m} & \cdots \\ \cdots & \cdots & \cdots & \cdots & \cdots \end{bmatrix}$$

In this way, each element of the matrix was formally linked to a transition between two atomic states, providing a fitting scheme to express the observable values of frequency and intensity of atomic radiation. Born, Heisenberg, and Jordan stated the rules for how to construct the matrices and manipulate them to obtain spectroscopic predictions. The details of this procedure are not important for the subject dealt with in this paper, but it is very relevant to note that these "infinite matrices" were no rigorous mathematical constructs. Born, Heisenberg, and Jordan manipulated them according to the usual rules for adding or multiplying finite matrices, but they fully acknowledged that for infinite matrices those rules led to infinite sums, which in all probability did not converge. For their aims it was sufficient that the physically relevant results obtained would make sense. In other words, the infinite matrices were a new medium of quantum theoretical practice through which predictions could be obtained.

In late 1925 Born collaborated with the already renowned mathematician Norbert Wiener (1894–1964) to generalize the formalism of matrix mechanics into "operator mechanics," which would be both physically significant and mathematically rigorous. However, their attempts were soon preempted by the unexpected appearance in early 1926 of Erwin Schrödinger's (1887–1961) wave mechanics.

The Return of Differential Equations

As we have seen, the development of quantum theory had taken a path that led it further and further away from the differential equations that dominated classical physics. With matrix mechanics and Heisenberg's suggestion of discarding atomic orbits, the formal development had also produced quite radical physical interpretations. However, differential equations made a surprising reentry into the game with a series of papers published by Schrödinger in the space of a few months in 1926.[9] Schrödinger had found an exactly solvable differential equation whose solutions $\psi_{m,n,l}$ depended on a set of three integer and semi-integer parameters (m, n, l) which precisely coincided with the quantum numbers of the stationary states of hydrogen. This was an essential new development as far as predictive power was concerned: both in the old quantum theory and in matrix mechanics quantum numbers had to be derived from empirically based spectroscopic formulas like Balmer's and then inserted by hand into the theory. Schrödinger's equation instead allowed the derivation of hydrogen quantum numbers without making reference to experiment. Similar equations could be written for all atoms and, although they could not be exactly solved, one assumed that they would in principle allow the derivation of the energy levels of the atoms. In a sense, Schrödinger's equation was a very complex and redundant apparatus to derive quantum numbers, and the question now was how its many parts could or should be interpreted physically. It was a new medium of theory opening up a huge new space of physical-mathematical speculation.

Schrödinger was understandably convinced that atomic spectroscopy might be reformulated in terms of the functions $\psi_{m,n,l}$, which he interpreted as describing "matter waves." However, the Schrödinger equation by itself could not deliver any spectroscopic prediction, as one still had to assume that quantum numbers corresponded with stationary states, and that "quantum jumps" between states would lead to radiation. As is well known, Schrödinger made it his main task to get rid of quantum jumps by appropriately extending his theory, but was never able to do so.

By 1927 the refined, if somehow still fragmentary, theoretical apparatus of quantum mechanics was in place, and it comprised Schrödinger's equations and their solutions, infinite matrices, and a verbally expressed statement about "quantum jumps" between "stationary states," which had originally been introduced by Bohr. The interpretation of the new theory was still quite fluid, and some features of Schrödinger's equations provided material for discussion.

A very important feature of the equation was the fact that if two functions solved it, then any linear combination of the two would be a solution, too. If a combination of two stationary states was also a solution, did this mean that an atom could be in two stationary states at the same time? Schrödinger had no problem with this view, since for him the "states"

---

9   For an overview of the early development of wave mechanics see Jammer (1966, 236–280).

were nothing but waves in a "matter field," and two waves could always be superimposed. Other authors however disagreed, among them Born, who suggested that the quantum wave should be interpreted as giving the probability with which an atom was in one or another state: "an atomic system can only ever be in a stationary state [...] but in general at a given moment we will only know that [...] there is a certain probability that the atom is in the n-th stationary state" (Born 1927, 171).[10]

This was an early statement about the "statistical interpretation" of quantum mechanics, and it marked the start of discussions on whether the idea of wave-particle duality that had been assumed for light quanta (i.e., photons) could and should also be regarded as valid for electrons and protons.[11] We see here how the (re)introduction of the classical medium of theory, differential equations, and function led to new physical questions. These in turn prompted scientists to further analyze quantum mechanics, both by trying to reframe it into more rigorous, unitary mathematical terms, and by attempting to establish experimentally which interpretation of the formalism—if any—made more sense.

Today, wave-particle duality is part of the standard interpretation of quantum mechanics, and the "two-slit experiment" appears in most textbooks as the paradigmatic exemplar of the experimental consequences of this duality. As shown by Kristel Michielsen and Hans De Raedt in this volume, however, the two-slit experiment was formulated only much later as a thought experiment, and actually performed even later. If one looks at what was happening in the 1920s and '30s, the situation appears much less clear than what may seem today. For example, in 1928 Arthur Edward Ruark (1899–1979) proposed, "A critical experiment on the statistical interpretation of quantum mechanics" (Ruark 1928). Ruark's proposal was an experiment that at the time could not be performed, aimed at establishing whether a single atom could actually be in two states at the same time: if that was the case, claimed Ruark, then the atom might be able to emit light of two frequencies at the same time. This idea sounds quite strange today, but these reflections belonged to an earlier, fluid state of quantum mechanics in which the wave function was still regarded as a novel formal construct, which helped formulate predictions but was not necessarily physically significant in itself.

10   "ein atomares System [ist] stets nur in einem stationären Zustand [...] im allgemeinen werden wir in einem Augenblick nur wissen, daß [...] eine gewisse Wahrscheinlichkeit dafür besteht, daß das Atom im n-ten Zustand ist" (Born 1927, 171).
11   On the emergence of the statistical interpretation of quantum mechanics see Jammer (1966, 282–293).

Dirac's Symbolic Notation

After this short detour on experiment, let us go back to the way in which quantum theory developed in the late 1920s. Most theorists were not primarily interested in interpreting the formal apparatus of quantum mechanics, but rather in expanding it to fit a broader range of quantum phenomena. Many authors worked to this aim, and their results often merged with and built upon each other. I would like to conclude my short media archaeology of quantum theory by focusing on one author who was probably the most creative one in his manipulation of symbolic expressions: Paul Dirac (1902–1984). In my presentation I have suggested that different authors contributing to the emergence of quantum theory used different aesthetic strategies to develop and express their theoretical research. Many of Bohr's key research contributions were expressed in words and not in mathematical language, while other authors, as for example Schrödinger, employed traditional mathematical techniques, such as differential equations. More skilled mathematicians, like John von Neumann (1903–1957), used very refined mathematical structures as guidelines for their work on quantum theory, while Heisenberg, Born, and Jordan expressed their reflections in the form of innovative, and possibly nonrigorous, constructs: infinite matrices. Dirac's strategy in theoretical research was the manipulation of symbolic notation without much regard for mathematical rigor on the one side or physical sense on the other.[12]

Dirac's papers, especially those he wrote early in his career, are often a challenge to read. Unlike Heisenberg or Bohr, he offered hardly any verbal explanation of the reasoning behind his operations, and unlike Schrödinger or von Neumann, his manipulations of mathematical symbols cannot be understood in terms of any sharply defined mathematical structure. Yet Dirac reached his most significant results by taking symbolic expressions and transforming them to generate new physical-mathematical meanings (Borrelli 2010). On the basis of archival material Peter Galison has argued that much of what Dirac did with his formulas was guided by a visual and haptic intuition, which he did not express in his papers—a "secret geometry," as Galison wrote (Galison 2000). While this may be the case, it is also clear that Dirac paid great attention to the development of a symbolic notation that fittted his aims. It was not a notation linked to rigorously defined mathematical notions, but rather reflected the way in which he wished to manipulate the epistemic objects he was creating.

---

12   On Dirac's transformation theory see Jammer (1966, 293–307).

In 1927, while the new quantum theory was proving very successful in dealing with atomic and molecular systems and discussions about its statistical interpretation were underway, Dirac published a paper in which he proposed an extension of quantum mechanics to the treatment of phenomena that were not discrete, like atomic spectra, but rather continuous, such as collisions between particles. For handling discrete systems, matrices were appropriate representations, in that the rows and columns formally reflected the discontinuous nature of the states— but what about systems where energy and other quantities varied continuously? Dirac neither described physical considerations in words nor followed a rigorous mathematical path, but rather tackled the problem in terms of finding an appropriate extension of matrix notation.

His idea was in principle simple: in atomic theory rows and columns of matrices corresponded with discrete energy states, but in a more general theory they would have to relate to states of quantum systems having continuous values of energy or other physical quantities. Dirac did not ask what mathematical structure might correspond to a generalization of matrices, as Born and Wiener had done, but simply spoke of "matrices with continuous rows and columns" (Dirac 1927, 625) and wrote down symbolic expressions for them that were not backed up with any rigorous mathematical notion. Let us look in some more detail at one example of his work.

As we saw, quantum mechanics contained infinite matrices, and in the standard notation the symbol $g_{a,a'}$ represented the element of the matrix for quantity g whose rows and columns corresponded to the values of quantity a. Dirac now introduced the symbol $g_{a,a'}$, which visually conveyed the idea that it was the same as the matrix for g, but with continuous rows and columns. Matrices could be manipulated by sums of their elements, and Dirac manipulated "continuous" matrices in an analogous way using integrals. For example, the rule for multiplying two matrices g and f had the form:

$$(g \cdot f)_{a,b} = \sum_{a'} g_{a,a'} f_{a',b}$$

In the case of "continuous" matrices, the rule for multiplying them became:

$$(g \cdot f)(a \cdot b) = \int g(a, a') f(a', b) da'$$

When working with matrices, a necessary tool was the matrix usually represented by the symbol $\delta_{a,b}$, that is, a matrix having 1 on its diagonal and 0 at all other positions:

$$\begin{pmatrix} 1 & 0 & 0 & 0 & \cdots \\ 0 & 1 & 0 & 0 & \cdots \\ 0 & 0 & 1 & 0 & \cdots \\ \cdots & \cdots & \cdots & \cdots & \cdots \end{pmatrix}$$

This matrix was regarded as the "unity" matrix, since any matrix multiplied by it remained unchanged. What kind of expression could take up the same role for "continuous" matrices? It was here that Dirac introduced his perhaps most successful creation: the "delta function," often also referred to as Dirac's delta function. Dirac introduced the delta function in a paragraph bearing the title "Notation." I will quote the passage at some length: readers not familiar with the delta function need not try to understand what the characterization means exactly, but simply appreciate the tone of the text, which gives a very good idea of the nonchalant attitude Dirac had to mathematical rigor.

> One cannot go far in the development of the theory of matrices with continuous ranges of rows and columns without needing a notation for that function of a c-number x [NB c-number = complex number] that is equal to zero except when x is very small, and whose integral through a range that contains the point $x = 0$ is equal to unity. We shall use the symbol $\delta(x)$ to denote this function, i.e. $\delta(x)$ is defined by:
>
> $\delta(x) = 0$ when $x \neq 0$
>
> and
>
> $\int_{-\infty}^{+\infty} \delta(x) = 1.$
>
> Strictly speaking, of course, $\delta(x)$ is not a proper function of x but can be regarded only as a limit of a certain sequence of functions. All the same one can use $\delta(x)$ as though it were a proper function for practically all the purposes of quantum mechanics without getting incorrect results. One can also use the differential coefficients of $\delta(x)$, namely $\delta'(x)$, $\delta''(x)$..., which are even more discontinuous and less "proper" then $\delta(x)$ itself. (Dirac 1927, 625)[13]

Thus, Dirac thought of the introduction of the delta function as a question of notation: he clearly perceived his theoretical activity as the manipulation not of mathematical objects of physical quantities, but rather of symbolic

13   Readers familiar with the delta function will have noticed that what Dirac is defining here is actually what we today would refer to as $\delta'(x)$, but soon the labeling of the function was changed to the one usual today.

expression that carried a hybrid meaning. When the manipulation was completed, the results might be tested for mathematical soundness and empirical accuracy, and if the outcome was positive, all was well. This attitude can be found in many theoretical physicists, but Dirac brought it to a new level, and mathematicians heavily criticized the delta function especially until it was eventually given a rigorous definition.[14]

Axiomatic Definitions

One of the main critics of Dirac's delta function, and more in general of the flippant way in which the creators of quantum mechanics handled symbolic expressions, was von Neumann. In 1928 von Neumann published a seminal paper offering a rigorous, axiomatically defined version of quantum mechanics based on a notion he developed specifically for that purpose: abstract Hilbert spaces (von Neumann 1928).[15] At the beginning of that paper he criticized specifically the delta function, and wrote:

> [In the present quantum theory] one cannot avoid to allow also the so-called improper functions, such as the function $\delta(x)$ used for the first time by Dirac, which has the following (absurd) properties:
>
> $\delta(x) = 0$, for $x \neq 0$
>
> $\int_{-\infty}^{+\infty} \delta(x) = 1$[16]. (von Neumann 1928)

Other than Dirac, von Neumann saw the delta function—and also other symbolic expressions—as always carrying a mathematical meaning, and regarded it in this case as "absurd." Von Neumann was able to distill from the symbolic expressions involved in quantum mechanics some rigorous mathematical constructs, but ironically this success helped support the physicists' view that it was perfectly fine to play fast and loose with physical-mathematical expressions, as long as the final result was not incorrect: eventually, so physicists thought, some mathematician would come along and show that what physicists had done improperly could be done just as well in a proper mathematical way. Still today, even if a

---

14   The delta function is today rigorously defined as a distribution; see Jauch (1972).

15   For an overview on von Neumann's early work on quantum mechanics see Jammer (1966, 307–322).

16   Man kann nämlich nicht vermeiden, auch sogenannten uneigentliche Eigenfunktionen mit zuzulassen, wie z.B. die zuerst von Dirac benutzte Funktion $\delta(x)$, die die folgenden (absurden) Eigenschaften haben soll: $\delta(x) = 0$, für $x \neq 0$, $\int_{-\infty}^{+\infty} \delta(x) = 1$" (von Neumann 1928, 3). von Neumann's characterization of the delta function is the same as is usual today.

symbolic procedure appears questionable, its success is usually taken by physicists as an indication that it corresponds with a rigorous mathematical procedure that no one has yet had the time or inclination to discover (Borrelli 2012; 2015a; 2015b). This attitude has led to many significant physical results, but has also made the status of mathematical formulas as a privileged medium of theory increasingly stronger, as it helped disregard problems of rigor and coherence as temporary issues that would find a solution with time.

Epilogue: Bra and Kets

von Neumann's formulation of a rigorous, axiomatically defined mathematical apparatus for quantum mechanics was appreciated more by mathematicians then by physicists. Abstract Hilbert spaces eventually became the overarching formal constructs for defining quantum theory, but in physics research practice they were rarely utilized. The rather cumbersome formalism introduced by von Neumann in his papers found few, if any, followers, and his innovative mathematical ideas ironically ended up being usually expressed in terms of the "improper" notation Dirac had introduced in 1927 and later continued to develop further. It is worth taking a closer look at the evolution of this notation, as it provides further evidence of the importance of the aesthetic, in this case visual and haptic, dimension of (quantum) theory.

In his 1927 paper, Dirac had pursued his extension of matrix mechanics to "continuous matrices" by generalizing an idea that was at the core of Heisenberg, Born, and Jordan's theory: matrix transformation. The matrix associated with a given quantity g (e.g., position) with rows and columns corresponding to another given quantity a (e.g., energy) could be transformed into a matrix associated with the same quantity g, but whose rows and columns were associated with a quantity c, different from the original one. This was done by multiplying the original matrix by an appropriate "transformation matrix" T and its inverse T^{-1} according to the rule:

$$g_{c,c'} = \sum_{a,a'} T_{c,a}\, g_{a,a'}\, T^{-1}_{a'c'} \, .$$

For transforming matrices with continuous indices, Dirac simply wrote the symbolic analogous formula in which the sum was replaced by an integral, without worrying about what it might mean exactly in mathematical terms:

$$g(a, a') = \int (a/c)\, g(c, c')\, (c'/a)\, dc\, dc' \, .$$

This formula defined the symbol (a/c) as the continuous equivalent of the transformation matrix, a "transformation function," but left huge mathematical questions open. The matrix sum had already been problematic for infinite matrices, since it was unclear whether it would converge. Generalizing it to an integral without specifying what form the various terms included in it would have was even more problematic. However, the new notation had a very clear intuitive interpretation for readers used to working with infinite matrices. It is particularly interesting to note that the symbol (c/a) had no graphic equivalent in the formalism of the time. The symbol somehow visually and haptically suggested a matrix of which only the indices were visible—an object whose only aim was to substitute the indices a for c or vice versa.

One might be tempted to regard Dirac's procedure as an axiomatic definition of new physical-mathematical notions through the way they were manipulated, and in some sense that was what Dirac was doing. Yet he was doing it at the aesthetic level of symbolic notation, and not by employing the standardized logical-mathematical formalism of the time, as von Neumann would later do. One might claim a posteriori that abstract Hilbert spaces were already "implicit" in Dirac's symbols, but this would in my opinion misinterpret the historical constellation. At the same time it would also be incorrect to deny that von Neumann's axiomatic construction was largely building upon the constructs developed "improperly" in quantum mechanics.

In his textbook *Principles of Quantum Mechanics* ([1930] 1935) Dirac employed an only slightly modified version of the notation used in 1927 for transformation functions, but in 1939 he published a paper "On a new notation for quantum mechanics" in which he developed that symbolism further into the now ubiquitous "bra-ket" notation. In that paper Dirac explicitly stated the importance of notation (Dirac 1939), noting right at the beginning:

> In mathematical theories the question of notation, while not of primary importance, is yet worthy of careful consideration, since a good notation can be of great value in helping the development of a theory, by making it easy to write down those quantities or combinations of quantities that are important, and difficult or impossible to write down those that are unimportant. (Dirac 1939, 416)

The key idea of the bra-ket notation was to split the notation developed for the transformation function into two halves:

(a/b) → <a | b> which was the product of the bra <a| and the ket |b>.

As is clear both from their name and their graphic form, a "bra" and a "ket" were supposed to be combined with each other in a particular order, so that a haptic dimension joined the visual and auditory ones. Putting a ket in front of a bra was possible, but the resulting ket-bra would have very different properties from a bra-ket, as immediately conveyed by its peculiar appearance: |a> <b|. Readers familiar with the formalism of quantum mechanics will know that bras and kets today are regarded as representing elements of an abstract Hilbert space and of its dual, respectively, and there is no doubt that Dirac was exploiting those mathematical structures as a guideline, while at the same time avoiding any rigorous definition and leaving it to his new notations to promote useful, and to impede unimportant, terms.

Conclusions: Computer Simulations as a New Medium of Quantum Theory

I am now at the end of my overview of the many media that contributed to the construction of quantum theory: perspective drawings, simple arithmetic formulas, verbally stated physical principles, sets of numbers, the rows and columns of infinite matrices, differential equations, axiomatic logical-mathematical constructs and, last but not least, Dirac's innovative symbolisms such as the bra-kets. Each author was free to choose the medium best suitable to his way of working and, especially in the early period, attitudes about what may or may not be acceptable as a "quantum theory" were very flexible—as long as correct results could be reproduced.

Can the employment of computer simulations to reproduce the results of quantum experiments without making use of the machinery of Schrödinger's equation be seen as a practice belonging to the tradition of quantum theory I just sketched? It is my conviction that this is the case, and I hope that my presentation offered some material to broaden the discussion on that issue. I am convinced that computer simulations as a new medium of quantum theory might bring back some of the productive tensions present in early quantum physics.

References

Badino, Massimiliano. 2015. *The Bumpy Road: Max Planck from Radiation Theory to the Quantum (1896–1906)*. New York: Springer.

Balmer, Johann Jakob. 1885. "Notiz über die Spectrallinien des Wasserstoffs." *Annalen der Physik* 261: 80–87.

Balmer, J. J. 1897. "A new formula for the wave-lengths of spectral lines." *The Astrophysical Journal* 5: 199–209.

Born, Max. 1927. "Das Adiabatenprinzip in der Quantenmechanik." *Zeitschrift für Physik* 40: 167–192.

Borrelli, Arianna. 2009. "The emergence of selection rules and their encounter with group theory, 1913–1927." *Studies in History and Philosophy of Modern Physics* 40 (4): 327–337.

Borrelli, A. 2010. "Dirac's bra-ket notation and the notion of a quantum state." In *Styles of Thinking in Science and Technology. Proceedings of the 3rd International Conference of the European Society for the History of Science*, edited by Hermann Hunger, Felicitals See-bacher, and Gerhard Holzer, 361–371. Vienna: Austrian Academy of Sciences Press.

Borrelli, A. 2012. "The case of the composite Higgs: The model as a 'Rosetta stone' in contemporary high-energy physics." *Studies in History and Philosophy of Modern Physics* 43 (3):195–214.

Borrelli, A. 2015a. "Between logos and mythos: Narratives of 'naturalness' in today's particle physics community." In *Narrated Communities – Narrated Realities: Narration as Cognitive Processing and Cultural Practice,* edited by Christoph Leitgeb, Hermann Blume, and Michael Rössner, 69–83. Boston: Brill/Rodopi.

Borrelli, A. 2015b. "Die Genesis des Gottesteilchens." In *Erzählung und Geltung: Wissenschaft zwischen Autorschaft und Autorität,* edited by Safia Azzouni, Stefan Böschen, and Carsten Reinhardt, 63–86. Weilerswist: Velbrück Wissenschaft.

Dirac, Paul. 1927. "The physical interpretation of the quantum dynamics." *Proceedings of the Royal Society of London A: Mathematical, Physical and Engineering Sciences* 113: 621–641.

Dirac, P. (1930) 1935. *The Principles of Quantum Mechanics*. Oxford: Clarendon Press.

Dirac, P. 1939. „A new notation for quantum mechanics". *Mathematical Proceedings of the Cambridge Philosophical Society* 35: 416–418.

Faye, Jan. 2014. "Copenhagen Interpretation of Quantum Mechanics. " In *The Stanford Encyclopedia of Philosophy (Fall 2014 Edition),* edited by Edward N. Zalta. http://plato.stanford.edu/archives/fall2014/entries/qm-copenhagen/.

Galison, Peter. 2000. "The suppressed drawing: Paul Dirac's hidden geometry." *Representations* 72: 145–166.

Hentschel, Klaus. 2002. *Mapping the Spectrum: Techniques of Visual Representation in Research and Teaching*. Oxford: Oxford University Press.

Hentschel, K. 2008. "Kultur und Technik in Engführung: Visuelle Analogien und Mustererkennung am Beispiel der Balmerformel." *Themenheft Forschung Universität Stuttgart* 4: 100–109.

Hentschel, K. 2012. "Walther Ritz's theoretical work on spectroscopy, focussing on series formulas." In *Le Destin Douloureux de Walther Ritz (1878–1909), Physicien Théoricien de Génie,* edited by Jean-Claude Pont, 129–156. Sion: Vallesia, Archives de l'Etat du Valais.

Huggins, William. 1880. "On the photographic spectra of stars." *Nature* 21: 269–270.

Jammer, Max. 1966. *The Conceptual Development of Quantum Mechanics*. New York: McGraw-Hill.

Jauch, Josef-Maria. 1972. "On bras and kets." In *Aspects of Quantum Theory*, edited by Abdus Salam, and Eugen Wigner, 137–167. Cambridge: Cambridge University Press.

Krämer, Sybille, Eva Christiane Cancik-Kirschbaum, and Rainer Totzke, eds. (2012). *Schriftbildlichkeit: Wahrnehmbarkeit, Materialität und Operarativität von Notationen.* Berlin: Akademie Verlag.

Kragh, Helge. 2012. *Niels Bohr and the Quantum Atom: the Bohr Model of Atomic Structure, 1913–1925.* Oxford: Oxford University Press.

Ruark, Arthur Edward. 1928. "A critical experiment on the statistical interpretation of quantum mechanics." *Proceedings of the National Academy of Sciences of the United States of America* 14: 328–330.

Velminski, Wladimir, and Gabriele Werner, eds. 2010. *Bildwelten des Wissens. Kunsthistorisches Jahrbuch für Bildkritik, Bd. 7,2: Mathematische Forme(l)n.* Berlin: De Gruyter.

von Neumann, John. 1928. "Mathematische Begründung der Quantenmechanik." *Nachrichten von der Gesellschaft der Wissenschaften zu Göttingen 1927*: 1–57.

Discussion with Arianna Borrelli

Hans-Jörg Rheinberger: Thank you very much for your talk. The stage is open for questions, please.

Hans De Raedt: That was a very nice presentation by the way. So, I was always wondering, in a way quantum theory is nothing but linear algebra, and linear algebra was known since the time of Gauss. So why did it take so long for these physicists to realize that what they were doing was just a form of linear algebra?

Arianna Borrelli: Thank you. That is a very good question on the history of mathematics and physics. There are many historians of mathematics, including me, working on that topic. The answer to your question is that, in a sense, linear algebra has not been there since Gauss. If we think of linear algebra as abstract algebra, that is in terms of abstract Hilbert spaces and similar formally defined objects that were introduced by von Neumann... if we think of linear algebra in that sense, then there was no "linear algebra" before quantum theory. There were only what we see today as different implementations of abstract linear algebra, like in differential equations or matrix calculus.

Now, if historically at a certain time there is no formalized, abstract linear algebra, the historical actors clearly could not use it to connect all the different "implementations." Take the example of infinite matrices: we can think of them in terms of abstract algebraic structures, as "operators" in Hilbert space. But the historical actors saw them differently. John von Neumann, for example, or David Hilbert thought that if you have an infinite matrix which is bounded, then that is a mathematical object and you can do linear algebra with it. But if you have an infinite matrix which is not bounded, like those of quantum mechanics, a matrix about whose behavior you can say nothing, then that is not a mathematical object—I mean, it may be a mathematical object today for me or for you, but for the people at the time, such a matrix was not a mathematical object. And so one could not do any algebra with it.

In a way one may speak of a "thought collective" in Ludwik Fleck's sense (Fleck 1935). What seems obvious to us was not obvious to the "thought collective" of quantum physicists at the time.

HDR: Is it historically correct that Heisenberg, when he was writing down this so-called matrix algebra, was not aware of the fact that he was doing that?

AB: Yes, this is correct for the first paper, the one written by Heisenberg alone. The matrix formulation was brought in by Born and Pascual Jordan, who were familiar with the matrix formulas. However, Heisenberg was working with a formal analogy to Fourier series and the multiplication of Fourier series by convolution. That procedure has the same form as matrix multiplication. So it's again a question of how you want to look at it. Born and Jordan replaced the structure of Fourier series with matrices. That's a very interesting story and in a way it also shows how a formula is not just a formula: the same formula can have completely different meanings for different authors.

Martin Warnke: Thank you, this was really a very enlightening presentation about how contingent the ways are to grasp the phenomena by different formal methods. But what really struck me was that you reiterated the fact that the double-slit experiment was so late in conception and in practice. So this is really something that is not clear to me: Why this came so late? But the question now is: Have you any clue about the nature of this experiment? Since if, as we both do, we follow Dirac in saying that the apparatuses and experiments evoke what they measure, how could that be, that there is one experiment and one apparatus that evokes those complementary phenomena at the same time? Is it a sort of joined—linked—experiment and thought experiment around which everything we do, did yesterday, and are doing today is orbiting?

Have you got any clue about that?

AB: First of all I have to say when I was preparing this presentation I looked for some history of the double-slit experiment, but there is none yet—and I think someone should write it! What I can say now—and maybe those who have worked more with the experiment can say more about this—is that in this early period there was a lot of open discussion about how to... what term did you use? "Evoke", yes? So, the physicists had these equations and wanted to try to evoke something from them. The question is: What? What were they interested in "evoking" through the equations? We now think of particles or waves, but that was not the case then.

For example, Ruark, he saw these equations as a possible indication of the nonconservation of energy. Ruark thought of the Schrödinger equation as possibly saying that energy is only statistically conserved, that you could look and find evidence of energy nonconservation in single events—but that in the end it would average out. He was trying to think of a critical experiment showing whether there was or was not this nonconservation. That's what he was trying to "evoke," if you want: energy conservation or its opposite.

In the late 1920s people were trying to use thought experiments to better grasp what exactly the theory could or could not mean. And maybe the idea for the double-slit experiment could only come afterwards, when somehow the notion of particle-wave duality became more prominent. Only then one thought of an experiment evoking waves or particles.

Kristel Michielsen: I have one comment. There is a paper (Rosa 2012) that you could consider as an historical overview of these double-slit experiments. It appeared actually because of a discussion on whether a Japanese or an Italian group was the first to do the real electron double-slit experiment.

AB: Thank you!

KM: And then related to your question or comment, Martin, I would say in the two-slit experiment the wave and the particle do not appear at the same time. Because you see single events coming and then there's still no observation of wave character, and you have to wait for quite some time before you see the interference. So it's not at all a simultaneous appearance of waves and particles.

Lukas Mairhofer: I also rather have a comment, because I think that really with the diffraction from a crystal you could demonstrate that there is some wave nature of things that you always have been thinking of as particles. So maybe the double-slit experiment is not that big a step as you seem to describe it. Because there is also an interference phenomenon, the diffraction from a crystal, and putting in a double slit is just creating a different apparatus for doing interference experiments.

MW: But we are just talking about interferences, now. We are not talking about the other side, the particle. You are talking about the bra and not about the ket.

Eric Winsberg: Yeah, no I agree with you, I think the double-slit experiment is pedagogically beautiful in the sense that you don't really have to know very much about other physics to see both the particle and the wave existing in the same experiment. But yeah, there are experiments that are harder to understand, where you have to have more arguments that maybe, you know, a sophomore undergraduate can follow. But yeah, I think there really are experiments like that.

HDR: One more question: On your last slide you said that if you do computations we need the wave function collapse. I actually don't think that is true. You said "wave functions, wave collapse is still needed for the computation." Wave functions, certainly, but wave collapse, it is not needed: there is no computation where you actually use it—interpretation, yes.

AB: Well, I was referring to having first a formula with abstract Hilbert spaces and then at some point, when you have to do the measurement, you have to introduce the wave functions, and then the collapse, in that only one component wave function is left after the measurement, and that gives you the probability of the results. So you are right: one does not compute with the wave collapse, but assumes it to explain how you arrive at the prediction for the probabilities. So it is indeed interpretation.

Frank Pasemann: So perhaps just one comment on Dirac's delta: of course it is precise mathematics today, it is a simple example of distribution theory. Now because it's about history perhaps I can give a small story. It was on the occasion of Dirac's eightieth birthday, where almost every still living physicist of that time gathered together to celebrate his birthday at the International Centre for Theoretical Physics in Trieste, and there was a talk by van der Waerden, I think at that time a famous mathematician, on Schrödinger equation history. He mentioned a physicist in Dublin named Cornelius Lanczos, and he worked out that he had exactly the same equation and the difficulties with interpretation, and he was arguing that because he was not embedded in the famous German school with all the discussion on how to interpret it, he was not—you know—as famous as Schrödinger.

Now at the end of this talk I think Jürgen Ehlers, director of the Max Planck Institute of Physics in Munich at that time, stood up and said, "I'm happy to introduce Lanczos here, who is around." And so he was still living, was a very old man with very long white hair, and it was very funny, you know, that someone stood up and that's the guy who had a talk about himself and no one knew that he was still living. Okay.

Anne Dippel: I have one last question. You said at the end computer simulations are another medium and they could bring back the tensions, the creative tensions, into theory. How would you relate your statement to the talk we had yesterday by Hans De Raedt and Kristel Michielsen?

AB: Yes, I think computer simulations could play a similar role to Dirac's strange notation. It would be an example of a different strategy to represent or to make contact with the experimental results—a strategy that has already produced these tensions with respect to the usual representation in terms of Schrödinger equations. I think this was quite clear in the discussion yesterday. It was strange: the discussion took the form of classical physics against quantum mechanics, and the Bell inequality—and these are... I don't want to say old subjects, but these are discussions that have been spoken about a lot. I think that there is actually more. I believe that in what Hans and Kristel presented there is some new dimension from the point of view of a representation.

And this is to me similar to the strange notations of Dirac—of course in a completely different way, but from the epistemic point of view similar. Of Dirac's notation today we can say: "Oh, we have now shown that it was rigorous." But then, at the time, much of what Dirac was doing was not rigorous. And it was just different from the mainstream, it was the path that he had to take, in a sense, to try and expand the theory that was there. But this is just my take on it.

References

Fleck, Ludwik. 1935. *Entstehung und Entwicklung einer wissenschaftlichen Tatsache: Einführung in die Lehre vom Denkstil und Denkkollektiv*. Frankfurt am Main: Suhrkamp; English translation: Trenn, Thaddeus J., and Robert K. Merton, eds. 1979. *The Genesis and Development of a Scientific Fact*. Chicago: University of Chicago Press.
Rosa, Rodolfo. 2012. "The Merli–Missiroli–Pozzi Two-Slit Electron-Interference Experiment." *Physics in Perspective* 14 (2): 178–195.

7

On Nature, its Mental Pictures and Simulatabilty: A Few Genealogical Remarks

Wolfgang Hagen

In a chapter titled "Scientific Imagination," Richard Feynman in his *Lectures on Physics* asked: What do I imagine when I see electromagnetic waves?

> What do *I* actually see? What are the demands of scientific imagination? Is it any different from trying to imagine that the room is full of invisible angels? No, it is not like imagining invisible angels. It requires a much higher degree of imagination to understand the electromagnetic field than to understand invisible angels. Why? Because to make invisible angels understandable, all I have to do is to alter their properties a little bit ... which is ... relatively easy. So you say, 'Professor, please give me an approximate description ...' —I'm sorry, I can't do that for you. ... When I start ..., I speak of the E- and B fields and wave my arms ... I see some kind of vague shadowy, wiggling lines—here and there is an E and B written on them somehow, ... I have a terrible confusion between the symbols I use to describe the objects and the objects themselves. I cannot really make a picture that is even nearly like the true waves. .... Perhaps the only hope, you say, is to take a mathematical view. ... From a mathematical view, there is an electric field vector and a magnetic field vector at every point in space; ... there are six numbers associated with every point. Can you imagine six numbers associated with each point in space? That's too hard. Can you imagine even one number associated with every point? I cannot! I can imagine such a thing as the temperature at every point in space. That seems to be understandable.

> There is a hotness and coldness that varies from place to place. But
> I honestly do not understand the idea of a number at every point.
> (Feynman 2006, 10-20)

This is the Feynman of the early sixties, lecturing undergraduates at
Caltech. We don't find a word about Bell's inequality, because these pre-
conditions for any experimental proof of quantum entanglement were
still unknown to physicists at that time. The *EPR (Einstein-Podolsky-Rosen)
paradox* is mentioned explicitly by Feynman though, in the end explained in
an original way by the uncertainty principle (Feynman 2006, 8-18).

But this is not the reason why I quoted this angel statement of Feynman, of
wiggling in the air and seeing numbers in space. What interests me is firstly,
that Feynman comes up with a question of "what is"; secondly how he
thereby embraces "scientific imagination"; thirdly how he incites solving the
problem; and finally how peculiar and odd he is talking about this topic.

To put it in more general terms: depicting electromagnetic waves, as this
little sketch already shows, is a question of how they are rendered. And,
if that is true, I would like to argue that they should be rendered as an
ontological, phenomenological, symbolical, epistemological, and also an
ethical or meta-ethical problem.

Ontologically one has to admit electromagnetic waves have a reality, but
a very special one, possibly in the way Niels Bohr spoke about "different
levels" of reality, where "conceptions like realism and idealism find no place
in objective description as we have defined it" (Bohr 1958, 89).

Phenomenologically there can be no doubt: at least as much as real entities
these waves are phenomena. As George Greenstein reminds us, "an electromagnetic wave is detected by monitoring its effect on charges—charges
in, for instance, an antenna" (Greenstein and Zajonc 1997, 83).

Thus detected as phenomena in reality, from the outset electromagnetic
waves have been shaped as symbolic mathematical descriptions rather
than empirical experiences. As is well known, Feynman's six numbers at
every point in space apply to Maxwell's equations which, as I will show you
soon, guided Hertz's experiments to success.

On this realistic, phenomenological, and symbolic level electromagnetism
has to be understood as an object and subject of a new scientific setting,
opening up a new epistemology—as Karen Barad puts it, as "a nondualistic
whole marking the subject-object boundary." Or with Bohr's words:
different to "the scope of classical physics, where the interaction between

object and apparatus can be neglected ..., in quantum physics this inter-action thus forms an inseparable part of the phenomenon" (Barad 2007, 136).

Eventually, concerns about ethics just draw the consequences of what I said about the epistemology, reality, and phenomenology of electromag-netism. As much as it comprises, on a basic quantum level, fundamental interactions between particles and wave mechanisms, electromagnetism has been responsible, over the last 120 years, for the groundbreaking successes of all new medial cultural techniques on a technological level. Electromagnetism, from the moment it came into existence as a technical phenomenon, encapsulates, in the sense of Donna Haraway, a long story in itself, still ongoing by the way, because it would never have come into existence and never would have grown to such worldwide dominance outside the subject-object connection of cultural techniques, nor outside the material, economically driven nature-culture discourses of scientific practice. According to Bohr, as Barad resumes: "The central lesson of quantum mechanics is that we are part of the nature that we seek to under-stand" (ibid., 265).

Not just John von Neumann's solutions of the quantum mechanical measurement problems, as I have shown elsewhere (Hagen 2002, 195–235), but already the basics of quantum theory itself have laid ground to the cybernetic feedback models in the sense of Norbert Wiener. In contrast to this, Barad emphasizes a new "ethico-onto-epistemic attention to our responsibilities not only for what we know" (Barad 2007, 283) but also, of course, for what we don't know yet.

I.

My genealogical remarks start off with Heinrich Hertz, around Christmas Day of 1887. Experimenting in his lecture hall in Karlsruhe, its walls and ceiling luckily built purely of wood, he knew quite well that all the light fall-ing through the windows consisted of waves as it was known since Fresnel's legendary proof of diffraction in 1819. This was already knowledge taught in schools, but any connection between light and electricity was still more than dubious. Not until 1873, just 15 years earlier, in the second volume of his *Treatise on Electricity And Magnetism,* James Clerk Maxwell had con-tested: "We shall have strong reasons for believing that light is an electro-magnetic phenomenon" (Maxwell 1873, 383). Ten years later the two vol-umes were translated into German. Eventually, after one year of research, over Christmas 1887 Hertz had to fulfill this impossible Feynman task, the task that has made electromagnetic waves somehow visible and verifiable as identical with light.

I don't want to go into too much detail about why and how Hertz started off with all of this. It began, in late autumn 1886, with a famous "dipole" scenario: Hertz amplified a *Rühmkorff inductor* (a device generating continuous discharges) using two big condensers spilling out sparks, which are—this is Hertz's experimental setting—received through tiny sparks spraying off from little slits in his receiving devices of bare wire (Fig. 1).

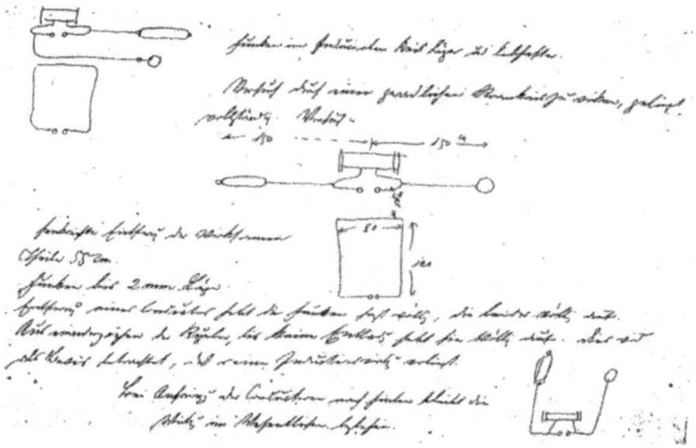

[Fig. 1] Foelsing 1997, 272

Let us remember that Hertz was part of the agent network of Hermann von Helmholtz, who held the most important post in German physics, at Berlin University, and who was very engaged in clarifying the fundamental differences between the German "nature-romantical" theory of electricity and the much more successful scientific approaches in the leading industrial nation at the time, Great Britain. To the dismay of the majority of German physicists, Helmholtz had translated Thomson and Tait's *Treatise on Natural Philosophy* as a students' textbook in 1871, explicitly lining himself up on the side of the British empirical theories against the prevailing Kantian transcendentalism in Germany. In those days Helmholtz gained the reputation of being a rude, materialistic thinker who denied the deep interconnections between the transcendental truth of nature and the human spirit, *dem menschlichen Geist* (see Cahan 1994).

As a matter of fact, one of the crucial points in this metaphysical dispute was the still open physical question of whether electricity could be a potential force with partly immediate distant effects, or if it should be conceived as a force of disturbances propagated by a so-called displacement current along conducting wires or without any carrier, traveling freely through space.

Of course, in these Christmas days, Hertz didn't see any electromagnetic waves at all. What he saw were sparks, only recognizable with special microscopic lenses, tiny little sparks oscillating in the slits of his receiver rings when he posted them on special points in his hall; luckily, as I mentioned, a room without any iron in its walls or ceiling, otherwise everything would have gone wrong, as so many failed replications of his experiments have shown painfully over the past decades (see Wittje 1995).

Entladung der Leidener Flasche,
intermittierende, kontinuierliche,
oszillatorische Entladung
und dabei geltende Gesetze

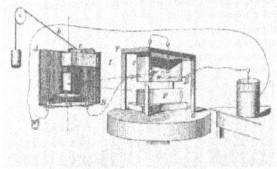

Abhandlungen
von
W. Feddersen
(1857–1866)

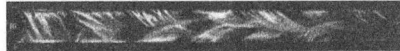

[Fig. 2] Feddersen 1908, Anhang I

Hertz's experimental setting was a spark-receiving circuit, extremely cute but also cumbersome. From the so-called Feddersen photo experiments of the 1850s (Feddersen 1858, 69–89) he knew a lot about the interior of discharging sparks (Fig. 2), namely that they include damped oscillations of alternating currents floating back and forth between the poles of the *Rühmkorff dipole*: "It has long been known that the discharge of a Leyden jar is not a continuous process, but that, like the striking of a clock, it consists of a large number of oscillations, of discharges in opposite senses which follow each other at exactly equal intervals." Interestingly Hertz considers this property a simulation, as he continues: electricity, to explain how it works in sparks, "is able to simulate the phenomena of elasticity" (Hertz 1896, 321).

Feddersen photos empirically affirmed the so-called Thomson formula of oscillation, $T = 2\pi\sqrt{(LC)}$,[1] and remembering that, Hertz knew roughly how fast the oscillations in his sparks were going. But, given all the elasticity, there seemed to be rather more chaotic happenings at the slit-pole of the receiving curls. Hertz knew that he could never compute the receiving spark frequencies there: their strength and brightness he could only observe with microlenses. One can imagine how tedious Hertz felt tagging specks on his floor plan (Fig. 3) where sparks looked brighter than elsewhere was.

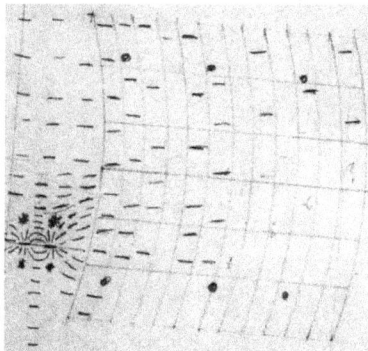

[Fig. 3] Doncel 1995, 222

Operating with metal mirrors and huge lumps of pitch placed between the dipole and the receiving rings, Hertz proved also in principle the similarities of electromagnetism and light in reflection and refraction characteristics. In the end, after one long year of countless tests, Hertz had a few rough calculations of the possible frequencies which, divided through the velocity of light, provided him with the theoretical length of his presumed waves. But, we are in a three-dimensional room and unfortunately, even Maxwell had not really entertained calculations of free propagating "disturbances" in spherical spaces. Above all, his mathematics was all but clear to his English contemporaries, let alone to a German physicist who was trained in the differential equations of Neumann and Weber potential expressions but by no means able to work with the quaternions and pre-vector mathematics Maxwell used in his treatise. The elegance of the four Maxwell equations

---

1   T = Period, L=Inductance, C=Capacity; the last two values Hertz could calculate from the parameters of his equipment.

as we know them today is in fact due to a reduction of about 12 in his book, work done by Josiah Gibbs and Oliver Heaviside after Hertz's death. However, Hertz's waves might look in 1887, elasticity simulating or not, they surely were not two-dimensional entities. So Hertz had to delve now into the very complicated mathematics of spherical harmonics in Maxwell's first volume, as his *Rühmkorff dipole* spilled out waves not in a linear plane, but rather curved in all possible directions. And above all, at a certain frequency, his waves peeled off and moved on as an autonomous electro-magnetic field, or just electromagnetic wave radiation.

At the level of contemporary scientific practice, nobody could know what was really happening here. Therefore Hertz had to grapple for something intelligible that could give him a picture of what was going on, an *inneres Scheinbild (mental image)* as he would call it later on. I will come back to that later. Indeed, he pictured to himself the inner processes in the discharge sparks.

"The period of a single oscillation" Hertz wrote, "is much shorter than the total duration of the discharge, and this suggests that we might use a single oscillation as a sign" (Hertz 1896, 321). Hertz wrote this two years later, telling the story of his experiments to the German Association for the Advancement Of Natural Science and Medicine. "Taking the oscillation which he couldn't see as a sign to identify something unseeable": this sentence I would like to highlight here, because it makes clear what Hertz was really concerned with. There were not only sparks he had to receive—he had also to solve an epistemological problem. His tiny sparks didn't just receive the big sparks of the *Rühmkorff*, although these were the phenomena. But for Hertz in every spark there was something unsee-able, like a furious mixture of abating frequencies caused by the damped oscillations, in every spark the *Rühmkorff* radiated. Feddersen's photos didn't show this "something" either, but gave at least a hint. Reproducing all the frequencies of a *Rühmkorff* spark on his floor-planes was impos-sible. Instead, here the *inneres Scheinbild comes* into its own: Hertz had to construct just one of them, one wave out of thousands the sparks radiated. He had to reconstruct one of them, estimating the length and shape of one wave, to get the points of the wave superpositions in his room (i.e., getting brighter receiving sparks to locate its shape more precisely in the room), and all this in the reality of thousands upon thousands of other waves of other frequencies swooshing around. In other words, he had to build up a precise and conscious intra-action between his apparatuses and the effects he wanted to identify.

"When you discharge the conductor of an electrical machine" says Hertz, "you excite oscillations whose period lies between a hundred-millionth and a thousand-millionth of a second ... There is still the possibility of success if we can only get two or three such sharply defined signs" (ibid.). The German original is important here: *scharfe Zeichen*. Please note this unusual German expression, actually a bit unclear. What is the sharpness of a sign? Clear and distinct, yes, but sharp? Maybe Feddersen and his view about spark photographs, is reverberating here. *Scheinbilder.*

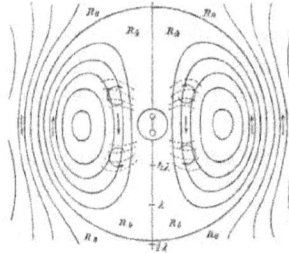

[Fig.4] Hertz 1893, 145

These now, two years later, are the harmonic spheres of Hertz (Fig. 4), very similar to what Maxwell has drawn in his *Treatise*. Seen from the strict perspective of Ernst Mach's epistemology, all Hertz had done was to make incorrect inferences. "For Mach a physical theory was no more than an abbreviated expression for a collection of statements about sense-data. Terms which could not be grounded in sensory experience were not to be retained in scientific discourse, and theories appealing to unobservable or indirectly observable entities—the electric waves of Hertz or the atoms and molecules of Boltzmann's statistical mechanics—ultimately were to be cast out as metaphysical superstitions" (Barker 1980, 247), as science historian Peter Barker put it. "Hertz on the other hand argued that ... at the level of experimental observation, the correlation of sentences in the theory with phenomena in the world is [strictly and only] imposed by ourselves, ..." Hertz's epistemology says that "a physical theory has a given structure is never a guarantee that reality has this structure" (ibid.).

That is to say: given the curves of Maxwell's theory, "we find as many points on the curve as we please" (Hertz 1893, 145). Let's be clear: Hertz is not faking his result. Although the curves are given here as a blueprint of his results, this is just one phase of his complex workflow. It is a phase and a part of his new intra acting approach to scientific practice.

For the last time, let's go back to the key device of Hertz and see what he has to say about how his mix of a simulative and experimental setting had worked out. "Just at the spot where we wish to detect the force" he explains,

> we place a conductor, ... interrupted in the middle by a small spark-gap. The rapidly alternating force sets the electricity of [this receiving] conductor in motion and gives rise to a spark at the gap. The method had to be found by experience, for no amount of thought could well have enabled one to predict that it would work satisfactorily. For the sparks are microscopically short, ... It almost seems absurd ... that they should be visible. (Hertz 1896, 322)

Well, nothing is absurd here. It's a mixture between thought simulation and proof from data. Most likely, Hertz climbed on his ladder only at those spots in the room where some theoretical computation in advance had already forecasted seeable sparks. Detecting sparks in an unexpected place would mean nothing, whereas not seeing sparks in an expected spot would mean at best a failure of the apparatus. Thus, Hertz performed a growing-in-practice and self-referential intra-action between his apparatus and the theory, proving, amplifying, and giving shape to itself in a feedback loop.

II.

Electromagnetism had to be discovered that way, or, to say it the other way round, in a Latourian turn: that's how electromagnetism produced its way of being detected. Let's keep in mind that Hertz didn't know anything about the interaction between photons and electrons: the discovery of the electron was still 10 years ahead, Planck's constant, the smallest quantum of action, 12 years, and Einstein's detection of the relativistic invariance of the electromagnetic waves another 18 years away. About 40 years ahead lay the definition of the uncertainty principle, Copenhagen complementarities, Schrödinger's equation, Dirac's *bra-kets* and von Neumann's *Hilbert space*. Nevertheless, Hertz's experimentation already shows rudimentary parts of the later quantum mechanical concept of nature. With and after Hertz nature is no longer an object of observation that remains untouched. Untouched nature, as Peter Mittelstaedt put it, is a nature "without relation to the possibility of observation" (Mittelstaedt 1986, 17 [my translation]). On the contrary, observation of nature in terms of physics is always a process of changing the observed, of constructing a new world of neo-ontological facts that are at the same time real phenomena, intelligible noumena, and subjects of empirical verification.

And, since Hertz, we have electronic media! Let's not forget, after the electromagnetic era of the telegraph, electronic media starts off with "Hertzian" waves, ironically in 1894, with Oliver Lodge's experiment in Liverpool, as a commemoration of Hertz's death. Electronic media, from radio telegraphy to the internet computer world, are based on quantum mechanically produced chips as well as on electromagnetism and the same epistemology, ontology, phenomenology, and ethics.

Regarding the medial side of his discovery, Hertz didn't anticipate it. Being asked by an engineer whether his "rays" could transmit telephone messages or something similar he replied honestly—no! Facilities for modulating electromagnetic frequencies up and down didn't exist in his time. And, he died before those weird folks like Edison and de Forest came around 15 years later, tinkering with light bulbs and cathode rays, not knowing what they were doing but thus inventing the radio tube.

Moreover, as a physicist Hertz had to cope with a far bigger dilemma. Electromagnetic waves demanded a medium for propagation, at his time called ether. His discovery seemed to affirm its existence insofar as one couldn't imagine how else these waves could propagate other than in a special medium. But, on the other hand, Hertz knew so much about the almost absurd qualities that this material should have, for example, absolute transparency for ponderable matter and at the same time an absolute density, even harder than diamond, thereby behaving totally elastically to propagate transversal waves.[2]

Hertz and Maxwell lived in the world of the ether absurdities, against which all possible inconsistencies of our quantum world look like child's play. William Thomson, the great hero of Helmholtz, had famously proposed his so-called *Vortex Atom Model* in the 1860s. While Hertz in Kiel and Karlsruhe had to teach Weber and Neumann "acting at a distance" electricity, George FitzGerald came out with his rotating model of ether molecules. After Maxwell published his theory in the 1870s, countless models came up of how electricity would travel through this rolling balls (see Nersessian 1983, 175–212). Hertz didn't live to see J. J. Thomson's electron detection and the subsequent plum pudding atom model of 1897 (see Keller 2013).

2   How familiar Hertz was with the ether theories of his time is shown in a recently found lecture from 1883: Hertz, Heinrich: Die Constitution der Materie: Eine Vorlesung über die Grundlagen der Physik aus dem Jahre 1884, Berlin: Springer, 1999.

My point is here, all these concepts, including Weber/Neumann's action at a distance electricity molecules (see Assis 1994), had one ontological assumption in common, and that is nature as a continuously comprehensive entirety, nature as an objective reality that doesn't jump. *Natura non facit saltus* had been one of the main principles of modern physics since Leibniz, who first coined this "continuity law": "c'est une de mes grandes maximes et des plus verifiées, que la nature ne fait jamais des sauts: ce que j'appelais la Loi de la Continuité" (Leibniz 1898, 110). Thus, Leibniz created a stable epistemological horizon corroborating the assumption that nature could be measurable with infinitesimal tools. More importantly, this same assumption allowed the subsequent emergence of a demand for a "completeness" of all theories dealing with a nature without jumps, called *continuity physics*. For instance, Heisenberg, still in 1955 referred to this continuity principle as if it was a cast-iron assertion. But, he gave a very "Bohrian" answer to the question of whether a quantum theory could still be considered in the realm of any continuity: "When the old adage 'Natura non facit saltus' is used as a basis for criticism of quantum theory, we can reply that certainly our knowledge can change suddenly and that this fact justifies the use of the term 'quantum jump'" (Heisenberg 1958, 9).

Long before quantum physics, Hertz took another course. After having done his heavy experimental year with electromagnetism, he started reconfiguring the relation between object and observer, subject and object, nature and culture, theory and practice. Explicitly and fraught with consequences. In the preface of his last book about mechanics we read: "We form for ourselves mental pictures [*innere Scheinbilder*] or symbols of external objects; and the form which we give them is such that the necessary consequents of the pictures in thought are always the pictures of the necessary consequents in nature of the things pictured" (Hertz 1899, 1). Again, Hertz is choosing his words very carefully; the German phrase *innere Scheinbilder* especially deserves a closer look.

Hertz follows Maxwell not only at the material level. He does it also in his epistemology, including a smart and almost inconspicuous renunciation of the continuity principle. "My theory," Maxwell had written, leads "to the conception of a medium in which the propagation takes place." We know that is the ether, never experimentally proven, but violently claimed and widely believed because of the continuity principle. "If we admit this medium as an hypothesis, I think ... that we ought to endeavour to construct a mental representation of all the details of its action, and this has been my constant aim in this treatise" (Maxwell 1873, 438). How smart. Maxwell conceived electromagnetic waves as ether waves, regardless of whether ether exists. Here we already see his careful decoupling from nature as such, conceiving a new theory of nature, which leads to the concept of a "mental representation"—surely the role model for Hertz's *Scheinbild*? Even if the continuity principle had been Maxwell's guideline, the question would have to be: what is the mental representation of ether besides electricity? Maxwell's answer: I don't have one, and I don't care. By the way, this is the reason Thomson rejected the ideas of Maxwell so strenuously.

The most striking thing to be found in Hertz's sentences might be the self-referential tone of his argument. To bestow pictures with an ability—as physical concepts—that their necessary consequences should always be pictures of the necessary consequences of the natural things pictured, weaves a carpet of paradoxes that can only be resolved by the perform-ance of a scientific practice. According to this theory, what is happening in observing nature is an intra-action of pictures with pictures, where the difference between one and the other is infected by apparatuses that encapsulate nature in a concept that Karen Barad has coined "agential realism" (Barad 2007, 165). The "certain conformity between nature and our mind" demanded by Hertz wouldn't work if nature is not part of our mind or our mind is an agent completely separated from nature. Indeed, this is a hidden variable, maybe the only necessary one in modern relativistic and quantum physics after Hertz, but if so then also, presumably, a new ethics is demanded.

"When from our accumulated previous experience," Hertz continues, "we have once succeeded in deducing pictures of the desired kind, we can then in a short time develop by means of them, as by means of models, the con-sequences which in the external world only arise in a comparatively long time, or as the result of our own interposition" (Hertz 1899, 1). I would like to call the reader's attention to the word *model*. What Hertz is outlining here can very well be understood as the concept of a simulation wherein we are configuring consequences that will arise in the external world indepen-dently of our ability to intervene appropriately.

In my view, the following sentence articulates the most striking and sur-prising thought of Hertz expressing an explicitly incomplete ontology, or to put it the other way round, an ontology of incompleteness: "The pictures which we here speak of," says Hertz, "are our conceptions of things; with the things themselves they are in conformity in one important respect, namely, in satisfying the above-mentioned requirement. For our purpose it is not necessary that they should be in conformity with the things in any other respect whatever" (ibid., 2). Let's apply this to the case of electro-magnetic waves. Do we—today—know they consist of particles called photons? Yes! Does that play a role in taking them as waves as it is proven in all known diffraction and refraction experiments? No! "We do not know," says Hertz, "nor have we any means of knowing, whether our conceptions of things are in conformity with them in any other than this one fundamental respect" (ibid.). Unfairly enough, I here recall debates about complementarity as they were held decades later in the 1920s. But, from the outset, Hertz pleads explicitly for an ethic of not knowing, since we will never know what nature "in itself" would be. There is no continuity principle anymore in the world view of Hertz's scientific thinking.

"As whether only matter exists and force is a property of it," adds one of the biggest fans of Hertz, "or whether force exists independently of matter or conversely whether matter is a product of force ... none of these questions are significant since all these concepts are only mental pictures whose purpose is to represent phenomena correctly" (Boltzmann 1974, 104). Again, referring to Barad's agential realism, with Ludwig Boltzmann we are in the same epistemological boat. The only existing things in nature are phenomena produced by a scientific practice led by mental pictures and symbols, but these phenomena are also enacted and acted out by nature. This is surely an idea of Bohr's, whose work is impressively resumed in the propositions of Barad, but which is also already present in the scientific thought of Boltzmann as a reader of Hertz.

The young Ludwig Wittgenstein was an intense reader of Boltzmann and thereby became acquainted with the thinking of Hertz. Wittgenstein adopts Hertz's vocabulary for his own account of the relationship between language and the world, as one reads in his *Tractatus Logico-Philosophicus*, written during the First World War:

> 2.1 We make for ourselves pictures of facts. [Wir machen uns Bilder der Tatsachen.]

> 2.12 A picture is a model of reality. [Das Bild ist ein Modell der Wirklichkeit.]

> 2.201 A picture depicts reality by representing a possibility of existence or non-existence of states of affairs. [Das Bild bildet die Wirklichkeit ab, indem es eine Möglichkeit des Bestehens und Nichtbestehens von Sachverhalten darstellt.]

> 2.202 A picture represents a possible situation in logical space. [Das Bild stellt eine mögliche Sachlage im logischen Raume dar.]

2.0212 It would then be impossible to draw up a picture of the world (true or false). [Es wäre dann unmöglich, ein Bild der Welt (wahr oder falsch) zu entwerfen.] (Wittgenstein [1922] 1984)

Wittgenstein's pioneering role in the development of analytical philosophy is undisputed and yet his so-called *metaphysical atomism* is discussed in these circles very virulently, even today. This atomism refers to the thesis that the world as a whole cannot be pictured, but all objects and things we can talk of have an enacting part in the world, otherwise they wouldn't exist at all.

And finally, Ernst Cassirer. He opened up his main work *The Philosophy of Symbolic Forms*, with a definition referring to Hertz. "The new ideal of knowledge … was brilliantly formulated by Heinrich Hertz in the introduction to his *Principles of Mechanics*. … The concept of the 'image'," writes Cassirer,

> had undergone an inner change. In place of the vague demand for a similarity of content between image and thing, we now find expressed a highly complex logical relation, a general intellectual condition …. Its value lies not in the mirroring of a given existence, but in what it accomplishes as an instrument of knowledge. (Cassirer 1955, 75)

Last comment: with and after Maxwell and Hertz, electricity gained a powerful epistemological dimension, but thereby it lost its *Anschaulichkeit*, its clarity, its aesthetic dimension completely. No similarity between image and thing anymore, to say it in Cassirer's words. Today, a silicon chip, as the most important piece of electricity, is an entirely anesthetic and "anesthesial" (see Derrida and Kamuf 2014, 26) device in the sense of Derrida's use of the word. In silicon grids we distinguish electrons from holes, as Shockley told us,[3] although electrical holes have no existence physically. On the other hand, without it, without these "holes", nothing would work in any modern computer, although there is no such a thing as a hole. Nobody will ever "see" it. It has, if at all, a quantum mechanical meaning only. Do these holes represent the magic of modernity, whose aesthetic potential holds the promise of a reconciliation of man and nature? I doubt it. The same applies to the electrodynamical occurrences in an antenna, the interchange between electrons and photons generating one of these myriad of

---

3   William Shockley was one of the inventors of the transistor in 1948 and the creator of its theoretical description, *Electrons and Holes in Semiconductors: With Applications to Transistor Electronics*, New York: Van Nostrand 1950, IX: "The hole, or deficit produced by removing an electron from the valence-bond structure of a crystal, is the chief reason for the existence of this book."

electromagnetic waves that hold our world together—does anybody feel the magic of reconciliation here? I'm not sure. Starting with Hertz, we live, as Barad puts it, maybe for a century now, in "agential realities." But instead of reflecting, in plain language, their limits and obligations, we still dream of them as a universal nature where electrical sparks spraying out of our head would tell of our vivid soul. But that's not the world we live in anymore.

That brings me to the famous Einstein, Podolsky, and Rosen article of 1935 concerning the problem of quantum entanglement. "Any serious consideration of a physical theory," Einstein and his colleagues wrote, "must take into account the distinction between the objective reality, which is independent of any theory, and the physical concepts with which the theory operates. These concepts are intended to correspond with the objective reality, and by means of these concepts we picture this reality to ourselves" (Einstein, Podolsky, and Rosen 1935, 777). So far, this refers to the Hertzian lemma of 1894, but interestingly Einstein continues differently. "In attempting to judge the success of a physical theory we may ask ourselves two questions: (1) 'Is the theory correct?' and (2) 'Is the description given by the theory complete?'."

As we have seen, completeness is what Hertz and Boltzmann somewhat excluded from their theory, and it might have been one of their crucial arguments to get rid of continuity physics and its epitomes like ether. Maybe Einstein's recollection has an inkling of that, so he feels he should become more verbose now: "Whatever the meaning is assigned to the term complete, the following requirement for a complete theory seems to be a necessary one: every element of the physical reality must have a counterpart in the physical theory."

I would like to sum up my genealogical review of Hertz by noting that Einstein, in his objection to quantum entanglements, re-established the horizon of continuity physics explicitly. But this quantum discourse emerged from the same scientific work that Einstein owed his early theories to—and this work was forced to get rid of all continuity prescriptions epistemologically. Maybe Hertz did that for the sake of a better world? We don't know.

References
Assis, André Koch Torres. 1994. *Weber's Electrodynamics*. Dordrecht: Springer.
Barad, Karen. 2007. *Meeting the Universe Halfway: Quantum Physics and the Entanglement of Matter and Meaning*, Durham: Duke University Press.
Barker, Peter. 1980. "Hertz and Wittgenstein." *Studies in History and Philosophy of Science* 151 (3): 243–256.

Bohr, Niels. 1958. *Atomic Physics and Human Knowledge*. New York: Wiley.

Boltzmann, Ludwig. 1974. "On the Fundamental Principles and Equations of Mechanics". In *Theoretical Physics And Philosophical Problems – Selected Writings*, edited by Ludwig Boltzmann, 101–128, Boston: Reidel.

Cahan, David. 1994. *Hermann von Helmholtz and the Foundations of Nineteenth-Century Science*. Berkeley: University of California Press.

Cassirer, Ernst. 1955. *The Philosophy of Symbolic Forms, Vol 1*. New Haven: Yale University Press.

Derrida, Jacques, and Peggy Kamuf. 2014. *The Death Penalty*, Chicago: University of Chicago Press.

Doncel, Manuel G. 1995. "Heinrich Hertz's Laboratory Notes of 1887." *Archive for History of Exact Sciences*, 49 (3): 197–270.

Einstein, Albert, Boris Podolsky, and Nathan Rosen. 1935. "Can Quantum-Mechanical Description of Physical Reality be Considered Complete?" *Physical Review Letters* 47 (10): 777–780.

Feddersen, Berend Wilhelm. 1858. "Beiträge zur Kenntnis des elektrischen Funkens." *Annalen der Physik* 103: 69–89.

Feddersen, Berend Wilhelm. 1908. "Entladung der Leidener Flasche, intermittierende, kontinuierliche, oszillatorische Entladung und dabei geltende Gesetze," Anhang I. Leipzig: Kugelmann.

Feynman, Richard P. 2006. *The Feynman Lectures on Physics*. San Francisco: Pearson Addison-Wesley.

Foelsing, Albrecht. 1997. *Heinrich Hertz. Eine Biographie*. Hamburg: Hoffmann & Campe, 272.

Greenstein, George, and Arthur G. Zajonc. 1997. *The Quantum Challenge: Modern Research on the Foundations of Quantum Mechanics*, Sudbury, MA: Jones and Bartlett.

Hagen, Wolfgang. 2002. "Die Entropie der Fotografie.- Skizzen zu einer Genealogie der digital-elektronischen Bildaufzeichnung." In *Paradigma Fotografie. Fotokritik am Ende des fotografischen Zeitalters, Band 1*, edited by Herta Wolf, 195–235, Frankfurt am Main: Suhrkamp.

Heisenberg, Werner. 1958. "The Copenhagen Interpretation of Quantum Theory." In *Physics and Philosophy, Vol. 1*, edited by Werner Heisenberg. New York: Harper & Brothers.

Hertz, Heinrich. 1893. "The Forces Of Electric Oscillations, Treated According To Maxwell's Theory." In *Electric Waves Being Researches On The Propagation Of Electric Action With Finite Velocity Through Space*, edited by Heinrich Hertz, 137–159, New York: Dover.

Hertz, Heinrich. 1896. "On The Relations Between Light And Electricity – A Lecture delivered at the Sixty-Second Meeting of the German Association for the Advancement of Natural Science and Medicine in Heidelberg on September 20th, 1889." In *Miscellaneous Papers*, edited by Heinrich Hertz, 313–327, London: Macmillan.

Hertz, Heinrich. 1899. *The Principles Of Mechanics – Presented In A New Form*. New York: Macmillan.

Keller, Alex. 2013. *The Infancy of Atomic Physics – Hercules in His Cradle*. Newburyport: Dover Publications.

Leibniz, Gottfried Wilhelm. 1898. *Nouveaux Essais sur l'Entendement Humain (2e édition)*. Paris: Hachette.

Maxwell, James Clerk. 1873. *A Treatise on Electricity And Magnetism, Vol 2*. Oxford: Clarendon.

Mittelstaedt, Peter. 1986. "Der Begriff der Natur in der modernen Physik." In *Sprache und Realität in der modernen Physik*, edited by Peter Mittelstaedt, 11–20, Mannheim: Wiss.Vlg.

Nersessian, Nancy J. 1983. "Aether/Or: The Creation of Scientific Concepts." *Studies in History and Philosophy of Science 15 (3)*: 175–212.

Thomson, William, and Peter Guthrie Tait. 1871. *Handbuch der theoretischen Physik, Autorisierte Deutsche Übersetzung* H. Helmholtz und G. Wertheim. Braunschweig: Vieweg.

Wittgenstein, Ludwig. 1922. *Tractatus Logico-Philosophicus*. London: Routledge & Kegan Paul; Wittgenstein: 1984. *Werkausgabe: [in 8 Bänden]. Logisch-philosophische Abhandlung. Tractatus Logico-Philosophicus*. Frankfurt: Suhrkamp.

Wittje, Roland. 1995. *Die frühen Experimente von Heinrich Hertz zur Ausbreitung der 'Elektrischen Kraft'. Entstehung, Entwicklung und Replikation eines Experiments*. Oldenburg, Thesis.

Discussion with Wolfgang Hagen

Hans Jörg Rheinberger: Thank you very much for this fascinating historical path that you have made us follow. When I looked at the translation of "innere Scheinbilder," I found it particularly stupid to call them mental pictures. Why didn't you translate it as internal simulacra?

Wolfgang Hagen: I take the translations published wherever possible, so I don't have to correct them so much.

HJR: And then the other point is with respect to the introduction to this—to Hertz's textbook—I think talking about these "innere Scheinbilder" and taking them as signs, that's all plain Helmholtz in a way? That's Helmholtz's sign theory applied to the particular purposes that Hertz has in mind there, but he is, if I remember correctly—it's a long time I've read this introduction—also making the claim that there is not just one consistent set of "innere Scheinbilder": you can have many of them that can be taken as being equivalent to each other.

WH: It's not explicitly stated in the preface; maybe he worked on this later, I don't know.

Eric Winsberg: So what's the German word for...

WH: "Innere Scheinbilder"

EW: I thought "Gedankenbilder" was the mental picture?

WH: It's not "Gedankenbilder," it's just "innere Scheinbilder." Here we have the slide. Some translations used mental images and some used symbols. I'll show you the real source of it—it's Goethe actually, I found out. It's from *Theory of Colors*, obviously.

"I looked on the bright circle five seconds and then having closed the aperture saw the colored visionary circle floating before me." And the colored visionary circle, this is an English translation of Goethe, is in German "das farbige Scheinbild." It's actually what you discover when you look too long into a very bright light and then close your eyes and then you have this...

EW: And that's the expression Hertz uses?

WH: Yes, "Scheinbild," which is untranslatable into English because it's not an illusionary picture, it's wrong. "Scheinbild," it's a Goethe word, that's all.

EW: It's what we call an aftereffect in English?

WH: Yes, but it's not an aftereffect because it's Goethe's theory of colors. It's very romantic.

Anne Dippel: The first time this "Scheinbild" appears is in Plato's cave.

WH: But not in German.

AD: No, but it would be helpful to look up the Greek word...

WH: Very!

AD: ...and then from the Greek word you could come to the...

WH: Goethe.

EW: You have to translate it into "Scheinbilder" okay, from the...

AD: No.

EW: If you translate it from Plato it would be "Scheinbilder."

WH: The word is seldom used in German. So I looked it up with every tool I have, in all the digital libraries, and I only found this Goethe quotation, which is cited very often in many other books.

AD: I'm sure you could find it in Hermann Pauli's Etymological Dictionary or in Kluger or in Grimm. I am very, very sure that...

WH: Yes, of course.

AD: ... this word is described etymologically and then you find the first time it appeared. But double terms in German appear from the sixteenth century onwards, so it is a new term, it must appear around 1870.

WH: Interesting, that's a good explanation. It's a very interesting word, because it's so important.

Lukas Mairhofer: So since you betrayed us, I of course have to ask about Wittgenstein, and also because when you ended with Einstein I thought, well, where is it that this continuum physics comes in again on a more epistemological level? Is it maybe with Ernst Mach? Is that maybe one of the big frictions between Machian thought and the Boltzmann–Hertz approach?

WH: I don't know, actually. I can't answer the question because I would say that the prominence and the popularity of Wittgenstein and Cassirer—and their relation and reference to Hertz, making him prominent as well—is very important in this context. So Einstein for sure knew Wittgenstein and the Frege group and all that, maybe he knew Mach better. I don't know. But either way, the original Hertz was not read and the original theory of Boltzmann referring to Hertz was not known anymore.

The whole "Scheinbild-Theorie" was kind of thought of in the context of Wittgenstein and Cassirer, as it is today. But the most important point for me is not the "Scheinbild-Theorie" but the break with continuity physics.

John Durham Peters: So, okay, I'm not a physicist, I'm a media theorist...

WH: ...like me.

JDP: ...and it strikes me that what you found is ground zero of media theory, in which all the contradictory notions of media are actually combined in Hertz...

WH: ...that's right.

JDP: ...whereas before you've got the kind of natural element, like the ether, after the mass medium of radio, you're talking about the variety of semiotic practices by which we reveal reality. But I think the one you're most interested in is the fact that the medium is something in which we intervene and thereby represent at the same time.

WH: Right.

JDP: And so I guess my question is: what is a medium? And that'll be the question for the previous lecture as well. I'm still confused by this question.

WH: But you gave the answer. I mean Hertz's reflection on what he did is in a way media theoretical as well, of course. So you're completely right. And we have—I've argued in this direction for a long time already—that media theory, which doesn't exist: media epistemology is equivalent to quantum epistemology and even cybernetic epistemology, because the figure of feedback mechanism and the figure of the self-referential building of not only concepts but the interaction between apparatus and nature, which is conceived in cybernetics as well, obviously stems from this source.

Arianna Borelli: I usually try to avoid using the term media too much. I know enough of media theory to know that there are all new media. In this context and sometimes when I present this subject, I like to use this term medium, as you would say, to prompt thoughts to go in a direction different than if I would say representation or form, especially if I'm speaking to historians of science or philosophers, to point out that there is some dynamic there in this representation, it's not passive.

Martin Warnke: Well friends, thank you so much. Now having brought us to the point where we just don't know anymore about the difference between theory and simulation, would you still make any difference after, say, having given up the continuity hypothesis?

WH: No, epistemologically not, but maybe in a way Eric showed us yesterday, practically. Because simulation is a new field of symbolic practice, maybe algorithm practice, I don't know. It has to be defined as a new field of practice, and epistemologically it's equivalent to any mathematical theory of nature. But that is not enough of an answer for what is a good simulation. We have to think about a kind of taxonomy of simulations; I don't know. I was not giving a lecture about simulations, but there must be a kind of taxonomy or something, a kind of logical work on it; the epistemological question you asked me—I mean, this seems for me to be answered.

It's like Hertz says, I mean it's elasticity, it's simulating elasticity.

Frank Pasemann: Yes, I'm a little bit confused by the concept of simulation. Of course I would like to discern between simulation in the sense that you can simulate something in the world in your brain, from computer simulation, which is of course perhaps closer to the media thing. So one should keep these as different things, at least for me.

WH: Of course.

FP: Otherwise there is a lot of confusion.

WH: What would you say about quantum simulation in the sense of Feynman, done without computers? Done without tool machines?

FP: I mean it's just to be precise what you mean by that.

WH: That's what I say...

FP: Otherwise we get confused.

WH: We have to have a kind of taxonomy.

HJR: Right. Exactly, thanks.

EW: Just a quick comment about the EPR quote that you put up: my memory of this is a little bit murky, but I think I remember Arthur Fine (2016) saying that that particular passage about elements of physical reality was one that Einstein didn't approve of, it was Rosen's—he wrote that passage I think and it might have been added to the draft after Einstein had seen it, before it went to press.

WH: Really? Okay.

EW: He might not have been a big fan of that.

WH: I mean god is not dicing, right?

EW: What's that?

WH: God is not dicing.

EW: Yeah, yeah.

WH: Playing with dice, so it's a continuity statement as well.

HJR: So absolutely, an atomistic statement. Very strange.

AD: I have two questions: I would love to hear something about that ethical dimension; and the second, it is very, very interesting what you said about the meaning of the image and the "Scheinbild" in mind and nature and so on. But when you look at actual physics practice, not in quantum mechanics, but in other fields, like high energy physics, the image itself is not important anymore as a device inside nature.

WH: But the simulation is important.

AD: The simulation is important.

WH: This is the image part.

AD: So you would just translate the digits and the algorithms and say that's equal to images?

WH: Of course.

AD: ...and there's no distinction between the algorithmic image and the visual image, because it seems to me there is a big distinction and that humans make sense out of that, and it's easier for us to somehow interpret images compared to letting the machine do the work, the medium doing the work of interpretation.

WH: That's right but we program the machine, as long as we are dealing with Turing machines, so there is the image part in it for me. Creating an algorithm is a way of creating images, so to say, because what is an image, on the other hand? What is a picture, on the other hand? Actually we don't know.

AD: Okay, got that. The second thing is you mentioned those examples from the natural sciences in the nineteenth century where the idea of a continuous or unified worldview somehow breaks apart, and that is something we observe not only in physics but we observe it in many, many other domains, in philosophy and so on. And then you show us how this need for some homogeneous description of the world returns through this. What kind of symptom is that? Wasn't it a liberating situation that Hertz detected, and how do you describe this constant urge and need of people to find some unified theory, when the world isn't unifiable according to what Hertz stated from logical reasoning?

WH: I don't know. I mean: have a guess! Maybe there are political reasons, or maybe economical reasons, to have a separate realm of nature only physicists can work on. I mean I don't know what the reason is to come back to continuity, to the physics of continuity or to a nature that is an entirety.

AD: Well, that was a power practice then in the end.

WH: Power, power may be one—maybe some other—I don't know, I mean I have to think about that, like you. But what I can say is that Hertz took another course and then he died, so to say. I mean that maybe electromagnetism as he found it took another course. I would just emphasize this Latourian picture of his experiments. You can say electromagnetism demanded this way of being detected. Know what I mean?

And this is a way we should think in the future, and therefore Karen Barad's approach is so interesting because she, in my view, is one of the first who radically thinks in a way that quantum physics and classic physics are not the problem, but the nature–culture relation in physics in general. So we have to think about that again under this perspective and from the start of the history of electromagnetism. Because for me electromagnetism makes a great cut into history. This is a real epoch break so to say.

There, in 1888, begins modernity, and not earlier, because electromagnetism is the first force, power, whatever, medium, we can produce in interaction with nature, so to say. It changed everything. I mean, just on a simple historical level you can see that. The industrial success and everything of the western world depended on electromagnetic techniques. And that's my point. We have to reconsider that under this epistemological horizon Hertz gives us. We have to really dig in under this horizon, and then we come to the point of ethics. Because there is a hidden variable, as I put it, between nature and mind, and there obviously is one, because there has to be a conformity, as Hertz says. Neumann would have described it—in his measurement chapter, which is very interesting—as an exchange of entropy and knowledge. That's his argument. In his measurement chapter, he says we can exchange entropy against knowledge. It's a very interesting thing. It stems from Fechner and this physio-psychological view of the world and things like that. Nobody invented something by himself. So, what I want to say is, this is kind of a part of physical thinking we should go back to, to discuss our problem of simulation of nature.

MW: What came back to my mind was that paper by Kittler (1991), where he says that computer simulations jump over the category and the register of imagination. I don't know what your opinion on this is. Then, we would have a difference between "innere Scheinbilder," because there are no "innere Scheinbilder" anymore, according to Kittler, if we would believe him. Because he says this is exactly the very nature of computer simulations, that there are no inner pictures anymore, this register is jumped over and left out. Would you think this argument has some reason to it?

WH: I wouldn't agree with your statement.

[To Kristel Michielsen and Hans De Raedt] I'm very interested in the source code of your simulation. Because I programmed for maybe 7–8 years in a row for other reasons, and the subjective experience I had was that programming is working with "innere Scheinbilder": you can't create an algorithm without having the imagination to think about how the machine works. So, what else is it than an "inneres Scheinbild"? Because it doesn't exist. The computer you're thinking about—wired programming—doesn't exist. And that's a problem all the time, but you know what I mean. So, the performance of programming is exactly creating "innere Scheinbilder" in a mathematical and special structure. And, whoever did that, seriously, will agree. Right?

HJR: But I think the really interesting feature of this paradoxical formulation of "Scheinbild" is that it is deconstructive.

WH: Yes, right.

HJR: On the one hand, it says picture; on the other hand, it denies…

WH: It says "Schein." Yes, it's wonderful. Good remark.

Hans De Raedt: I fully agree with what you said about, say, the practice of computer programming and so on. But, maybe I would also like to make a bridge to what Martin says because, when we have done this… I'm talking about computing on a digital computer, we know that, at least in principle—but we can also do it in practice, although it is fairly expensive—we can build a, let's say, Lego machine that does exactly the same thing that our program is doing. So then, would you still call that a "Scheinbild"? So I have now a mechanical…

WH: That's an interesting question.

HDR: …device that is doing exactly the same type of thing. I mean, not exactly in terms of, say, basic things it does. But the final result is the same—things are moving around and so on. So it's really mechanical. We can clearly visualize it. I mean, it's a natural thing for us, and it does the same thing. So where are the "Scheinbilder" then?

WH: I thought about this tinkering. I mentioned Edison and de Forest, successfully, because they are building the radio tubes, which are so, so immensely important for the evolution of electromagnetic media. But neither Edison nor de Forest knew a thing. Maybe they worked with "innere Scheinbilder," I don't know. But, the main thing is, they worked with material. They did it. They did it somehow. They tinkered, they just practiced by playing around with things. This is not "innere Scheinbild." When I programmed, I couldn't play around with things. I would have liked to do that, but what I played around with was some things in my head, and I can't even describe them.

FP: And just as a comment I spontaneously would think the same thing. But when I talked yesterday about the explorative simulations, you can think about programming, creating new programs, and constructing systems you haven't thought about. And that's one of the interesting things today.

Britta Schinzel: To add to the "innere Scheinbilder" effect from logic recursion theory: we know that for every mathematical function, there exists an uncountably infinite set of infinite sequences of equivalent programs. So, you know that every "innere Scheinbild" produces a different program, a different source code.

HJR: Now things are starting to become messy and complicated at this point. Let us stop here, and thank our speaker for this stimulating discussion. Thank you.

References

Fine, Arthur. 2016. "The Einstein-Podolsky-Rosen Argument in Quantum Theory." In *The Stanford Encyclopedia of Philosophy (Fall 2016 Edition)*, edited by Edward N. Zalta, accessed January 26, 2017, http://plato.stanford.edu/archives/fall2016/entries/qt-epr.

Kittler, Friedrich. 1991. „Fiktion und Simulation." In *Aisthesis: Wahrnehmung heute oder Perspektiven einer anderen Ästhetik*, edited by Karlheinz Barck, Peter Gente, Heidi Paris, and Stefan Richter, 196–213. Leipzig: Reclam.

8

Intervention

Hans-Jörg Rheinberger

As announced beforehand, I will not be able to present a fitting, full-length contribution to this workshop, for two reasons: first, I am not a physicist and in particular not familiar with the mathematics involved in most of the argumentation of our preparatory reading; and second, I am not an expert in computer simulation either. Therefore I am actually here to listen to the specialists and learn from them rather than being ready to present my own work pertinent to the topic.

What I have always been most interested in as a historian of science is the question of how to describe and understand scientific experimentation and the shapes it assumes over time. For our purposes, it might be safe to start from the observation that the forms of experimentation span a broad space between two extremes. On the one hand, we have what could be called the demonstration experiment. You trim your experiment so that it fits, or fulfils the conditions of, certain theoretical assumptions that are being taken for granted. This is the traditional idea of an experiment as a testing mechanism. I myself have been more inclined to look at what Friedrich Steinle and others aptly call "exploratory experimentation" (Steinle 2005; Waters 2007). Exploratory experiments ideally produce knowledge that is not yet to hand, that is, genuinely new knowledge. The question is how experiments should be arranged and conducted so that they potentially give rise to knowledge that we do not yet have and could not even have imagined.

My interest is thus less in experiments designed to test consequences that can be derived from certain acknowledged premises, but rather in experiments that are designed in such a way that they allow for the potential detection of things that are not in the realm of the possible consequences of our present knowledge. This is precisely what conveys to the sciences their intrinsic historicity. Historicity is unthinkable without that element of contingency—not pure contingency, but a contained contingency of sorts. Let me relate at this point to the title of our workshop: this is exactly what I understand by the notion of "event." Experimentation in this sense is "eventuation."

My question in the context of this workshop is whether this distinction maps onto the two kinds of experiments described in the two papers that we were given to read. The matter-wave interference experiments might fit this latter description (Hornberger 2012). The question is whether computer experiments as described in the second paper (De Raedt, Katsnelson, and Michielsen 2014), which basically lack the resistance and resilience of matter to interact with as in real world experimentation, can do this at all. This is one point that interests me here. I would like to learn more about the concepts involved with *in silico* experimentation (see e.g., Gramelsberger 2010), and in particular the relation between laboratory experiments and computer experiments.

There is a longstanding tradition of what are being called "thought experiments." Does computer experimentation give thought experiments a particular shape and power? Or are they simply a means to test the consequences of certain mathematical assumptions, or to follow the deployment of certain algorithms, a tool to check virtual models as Jülich neuroscientist Katrin Amunts recently put it (see Zauner 2016, 16)?

There is another point I would like to briefly address. Reading the paper of Hans De Raedt, Mikhail Katsnelson, and Kristel Michielsen on "Quantum theory as the most robust description of reproducible experiments," (De Raedt, Katsnelson, and Michielsen 2014) I was intrigued by two things.

First, there is the plain and unmistakable rejection of any ontological commitment as far as the quantum behavior of particles—or more generally, matter—is concerned. "Quantum theory," the authors write by appealing to Niels Bohr, Max Born and Wolfgang Pauli, "describes our *knowledge* of the atomic phenomena rather than the atomic phenomena themselves" (ibid., 46). This is a radically epistemological statement. The question is: Can we generalize it? The first step would be to ask whether this would also pertain to computer experimentation. Computer models, say, of climate change, would thus describe our knowledge of the dynamics of the climate and not of climate change itself. The second step would be to ask whether we could include the scientific assessment of any macroscopic phenomenon as well, to the extent that *any* theory scientifically addressing the phenomena of our world would describe our knowledge—and test its consistency—of these phenomena rather than representing a statistical or cause-effect characteristic of the respective phenomena in question.

That would amount to the conclusion that scientific reasoning would be radically situated at the level of epistemology, including the measurements and counts that are being recorded as the outcomes of an experiment. These traces would always already belong to the level of representation, with the additional consequence that "representation" would be the wrong word to use in that context altogether. Ontologies in science would thus have to be qualified as metaphysical, following a tradition that goes at least back to Ernst Mach and his peers at the turn from the nineteenth to the twentieth century.

This latter point appears to me actually to be implied by the second claim of the paper that I found intriguing: that a macroscopic experimental setup with the characteristics described in that paper—"There may be uncertainty about each event. The conditions under which the experiment is carried out may be uncertain. The frequencies with which events are observed are reproducible and robust against small changes in the conditions" (ibid., 50)—can be given a quantum theoretical description. And in addition, that such a description is postulated to follow from ordinary reasoning in terms of logical inference. Does that mean, in the last consequence, that the distinction between a quantum level of description and a macroscopic level of description actually collapses? The following sentence appears indeed to indicate such a collapse: "Our basic knowledge always starts from the middle, that is, from the world of macroscopic objects. According to Bohr, the quantum theoretical description crucially depends on the existence of macroscopic objects which can be used as measuring devices" (ibid., 47). And the accompanying question is whether "our basic knowledge" includes "the principles of logical inference" (ibid., 46). The overall question is whether the argument can be summarized as follows: take an experimental setup with the above described (macroscopic) characteristics, apply the principles of logical inference, and you will arrive at a quantum theoretical description of the situation. Formulated otherwise: a quantum theoretical description is implied in and follows from a particular kind of experimental situation and the events resulting from that situation. The conclusion is that quantum theory would thus be a description of our very experimental way of knowing, if I see it correctly.

References

De Raedt, Hans, Mikhail I. Katsnelson, and Kristel Michielsen. 2014. "Quantum theory as the most robust description of reproducible experiments." *Annals of Physics* 347: 45–73.

Gramelsberger, Gabriele. 2010. *Computerexperimente: Zum Wandel der Wissenschaft im Zeitalter des Computers*. Bielefeld: Transcript Verlag.

Hornberger, Klaus, Stefan Gerlich, Philipp Haslinger, Stefan Nimmrichter, and Markus Arndt. 2012. "Colloquium: Quantum interference of clusters and molecules." *Reviews of Modern Physics* 84: 157–73.

Steinle, Friedrich. 2005. *Explorative Experimente: Ampère, Faraday und die Ursprünge der Elektrodynamik*. Stuttgart: Steiner.

Waters, C. Kenneth. 2007. "The nature and context of exploratory experimentation: An introduction to three case studies of exploratory research." *History and Philosophy of the Life Sciences* 29: 275–84.

Zauner, Hans. 2016. "Im Gespräch mit Katrin Amunts: Ein Modell allein kann das Gehirn nicht erklären." *Laborjournal* 10: 14–17.

Discussion with Hans-Jörg Rheinberger

Janina Wellmann: Thank you very much. Hans de Raedt, you want to answer first to the interventional questions of Hans-Jörg Rheinberger?

Hans De Raedt: Well, I'm not so sure. Too many questions at the same time; there's a lot of uncertainty here. I think what we try to show in the papers and data is that if you have these different uncertainties in the problem, and the way of collecting data is statistical, that it unavoidably leads to the kind of description that we now characterize as quantum mechanical. Whether or not you really then see the effects depends on the scale of the uncertainty versus the set of knowledge that you have, so to speak, for certain. But the structure of the theory is always like that; I think that is true. From a purely logical point of view, if you agree with the principles of logical inference, then the answer is it has to be the quantum mechanical description as a framework.

Lukas Mairhofer: Although I agree that we should be really careful about deriving ontologies from our theories, I have the strong feeling that you always have to assume something about the entities that your theory's operating on, that is on the logical level. Quantum theory doesn't tell us about the fundamental entities, what they are. It doesn't tell us, "Well, it's a particle." Or, "Well, it's a wave." But, it tells us that we should not think about it as only particles or only waves. That's what I think. And, to come to my question: What do you have to assume about your entities to logically infer quantum mechanics from microscopic classical physics? Because I don't think that you can. How do you get there?

HDR: So you have the paper there?

Hans-Jörg Rheinberger: Yes, I have the paper here.

HDR: If I remember well, maybe on the first page there's a quote from Bohr. You can read it, maybe, for us about what the aim of physics is supposed to be.

HJR: Yes. We have here three sentences that are ascribed to Bohr. First, there is no quantum world; there is only an abstract physical description. Second, it is wrong to think that the task of physics is to find out how nature is. Third, physics concerns what we can say about nature.

HDR: Okay, that's the one I want to have. So, the starting point of these considerations is exactly that we are not asking about what is, but only about what we can say. The starting point is the notion of the event, and event means the perception of the event that we as humans have. And, we can, of course, also start asking what is this? But this question we do not ask.

LM: But why not? Because to have...

HDR: Because we don't want to.

LM: But if you have an event, you already... I mean, you already ascribe to nature that it's possible to affect your senses. That's already not a logical statement. You cannot talk about... I mean, I'm completely with you that we should not put everything into ontology and that it is not the task of physics to teach us about nature. But, even if it is the task of physics to tell us about our perceptions, we have to assume, in our theory, some things about nature. I don't see how we can completely get rid of ontology.

HDR: No, no. But the paper is not against ontology, not at all. It's about how you reason on the basis of the information that you have about experiments. It is not against ontology. The talk that Kristel [Michielsen] gave is much more on the other side than this one. And there is no contradiction. There's absolutely no contradiction nor a conflict in these things. So, this paper is about how we can reason in the presence of uncertainty, and that is all it tries to do. And the starting point is then the data that we accumulate in the experiment. Where these data are coming from and whether there is an ontology behind it, which we don't know in any case, simply doesn't matter for the description. That is the message.

HJR: But the message is also that the kind of uncertainty we have on the macroscopic level is not qualitatively different from the uncertainty that you have on the microscopic or the atomic level. And that's a strong kind of claim.

HDR: So the underlying assumption in the whole story, of course, is that we never know everything. So, certainty would mean that for a given situation we are dealing with, we really know everything about the situation. Now, this is an assumption I'm not prepared to make. We always deal with situations of uncertainty. I'm not talking about real laboratory experiments whatsoever. Not about some mathematical theory. Because, in that case, of course we do know everything. It's hidden in the axioms. That's another situation. So we're not talking about this situation, we're talking about a situation where we have data that we accumulate by whatever means, say by looking at it or just registered by means of a computer or whatever. We have data and we want to make inferences based on these data. And then, completely in line, I think, with what Bohr was saying, is that in that case, quantum mechanics is exhausted in the sense that you cannot do better. It's the best inference you can make on the basis of the data that you have. In that sense, many of the experiments that are being done today, which are, so to speak, quantum experiments, are merely some kind of demonstration that people are searching for the conditions under which this is realized. And they have to work very, very hard to realize these conditions. If you don't have the right conditions, you'll also see something—why not analyze it? You don't, because you cannot. You see? You have no tools to do that. You don't see systematics—no.

Only in special cases you get systematics and so on, and what the paper tells you is that this is because it is the best. It is a kind of fixed point. It's an optimization in terms of theories. That is what the paper says, but it doesn't say anything about ontology. Not at all.

HJR: That was my addition.

LM: And I think my question was more directed to this addition.

9

Round Table

John Durham Peters: My question is that if the interaction of object and apparatus is at the heart of quantum physics, why is it that popular conceptions of what science is are still so connected to just grabbing on to reality as such with sense data? Why is that so hard to shake? That's my question.

Frieder Nake: I don't have a question. Is it possible for a regular human being to understand quantum mechanics?

Thomas Bjørnsten: I'm not sure that I have a regular question, but I can say, which some of you already know by now, that one of the reasons that I'm here is that I'm interested in the topic, because I'm doing research on data visualization. So, for me, a really interesting question concerning what has been discussed here: apart from all the aspects of quantum theory and physics that I don't understand, the interrelation of what we conceive of as visualization as opposed to or parallel with simulation is a puzzling question for me that I'm dealing with. So it's just to sort of mention that there's a discussion around this topic. The differences, the similarities, between the negotiation of visualization as opposed to simulation. This is what I'm bringing with me from here, which we may discuss further on at some point.

Lukas Mairhofer: I'm still hooked up a little bit on the discussion from before. So the question that's running around in my head at the moment is where does the uncertainty come from? Does it only come from our imperfect knowledge, or does it also come from the other side of the cognitive process? Does it come from nature itself? And then, of course, is quantum uncertainty really the same as macroscopic uncertainty? Because after all, there are very different statistics that describe these uncertainties. So where does the uncertainty come from?

Mira Maiwöger: Right now I'm mainly wondering about what I'm dealing with in my daily life, like my Bose–Einstein condensates in this lab together with this machine. What is this? Because after all, they kick back sometimes, so this phrase by Karen Barad, the world kicks back, which I was thinking about before in the discussion about the ontological aspects of us doing science. For me, this is sometimes mainly the ontology, I guess. Sometimes things just don't work out, the lab does not work or the experiment does not work. Or it works differently. There is this element of surprise.

Stefan Zieme: Okay, maybe I can give an answer now. I think quantum mechanics doesn't make any sense beyond the mathematical framework, and that's fine with me. I never dare to think about it at all. What do I care? It works out perfectly. It's the same with quantum field theory, and, if you continue that line, it goes into string theory, and there you are at a point where you have a purely mathematical framework. You could call it mathematical physics. What drives me is, how do you chart new grounds in mathematical physics where you don't have anything? You don't have any phenomena, you don't have any settings, you don't have any data, and you don't have axioms. It's not math. It's something very strange; I don't know what it is. There's progress, and I don't know why there's progress, but I like it.

Eric Winsberg: I think I probably said enough.

Wolfgang Hagen: I don't know. I'm a little bit struck because of this day, and I learned a lot. I'm looking for this question of ethics to answer somehow, because I found out that it is very important to talk about ethics in the realm of physical knowledge, so to say. And I would recommend to hold, very soon, a workshop about that.

Jeremias Herberg: I joined in late. It was great to hear you guys speak. One thing I can just share to maybe, in some way, contribute: I just wrote a chapter in my dissertation on how the notion of fields traveled to sociology, and how it became a "Scheinbild," maybe. And actually occupying an entire area of sociology with only one Scheinbild, Pierre Bourdieu, and how you could maybe alternate that with another Scheinbild. So that's only to add to this discussion that we just had on, in this case, social ontology maybe, and the way we look at it and the interaction between those things. That happens in the social sciences in a similar way without, I think, simulation maybe. I mean, sociologists today hardly speak about that. That's it.

Frank Pasemann: Well, I think I don't want to comment on quantum mechanics because I spent too much of my lifetime on that. But I would like to comment on something I still believe, and perhaps others also, that computer simulations can produce new knowledge. I showed you this Fermi-Pasta-Ulam problem as one of the first examples. But today, I think it's very clear why they call it exploratory simulations: it's that you really find new things. There are a lot of examples. Perhaps I can tell about my own way using this approach. As a physicist, looking into brain sciences, I saw all these very interesting fantasies about how brains work. But coming from outside what you learn first is that brains are oscillating and there is a highly recurrent connectivity between neurons. Everyone knows it. But the neural network theory was about input/output maps. And, of course, if you look at the recurrences and knew a little bit from cybernetics, you know that more interesting things must happen there, just because of the loop structure. One then may hypothesize that the capacity of biological brains relies exactly on these properties. Of course you cannot verify that on anesthetized cats or something like that. So I said forget it—I don't need this kind of knowledge. So what is the point? There is a hypothesis: Capabilities of brains rely on looping signals. And, of course, then you go to simulation and look for systems that have these loops. You then realize that there are too many parameters and processes to study, that there is no theory, and that mathematics can tell you almost nothing about the observed phenomena.

You only know there are very many interesting phenomena to expect, but you don't know what will be of relevance for brain science. That's why I came to robotics, assuming that to have a brain only makes sense if you have to control a body. Very many discussions were about results obtained from studies on dead brains, not reflecting the functions of living brains. So one may learn lots of things from exploratory simulations—for instance, that very different sizes of systems can all generate one and the same function. And then you may come up with new questions concerning stability of brain processes, plasticity of brain structure and all that. To have a test body for your simulated processes you may then use physical or simulated robots in real or simulated environments to control the boundary conditions of your simulation. Then I know what I'm doing, then I'm not fantasizing. So if you implement your results from this type of simulations to something which is real world like a robot, I think you can get quite a lot of new insights into how brain may work.

EW: Just very quickly, on the point about computer simulations discovering new things, there's, I think, supposedly announced a discovery yesterday of a new ninth planet. We got rid of Pluto—it's no longer a planet. They think maybe they found a new ninth planet using computer simulation. So, it seems pretty clear that computer simulation is...

SZ: Well, I guess we should pass it on, but I have strong objections to that. Just to put it on the list that you say there's a computer simulation on something. I mean, in 1846 Le Verrier did the very same thing. So what's not a simulation? You solve Newton's equations with some perturbations, and the solution doesn't work out, so he had a world view, he had a paradigm. He made a choice, he followed the path, something was left over, he experimented—with a mathematical tool, of course—but, to my belief, this is not a simulation. If you put it on a computer, you can do it on pen and paper when you're good, or you can put it on a computer. That's your choice. But I wouldn't call that a simulation.

Kristel Michielsen: Okay, so I have a question, and maybe it is more to the historians of science. My question is, I have the impression that, at this moment, the atmosphere, at least in quantum physics, is such that experimenters are trying to measure what theory predicted or has given, and unknown facts are simply thrown away because they don't have an explanation for them. And, as a consequence of this, by doing computer simulations, by playing around with computer simulations, we could maybe find new things. But the atmosphere is such that they're then considered to be strange, even not willing to test because they do not fit into the picture. So, my question is, why is this? Was this also the case maybe when they started to think about quantum theory as a new theory?

Hans De Raedt: Did you see similar things in biology?

KM: Yeah, because you have a very nice example that you suddenly find something new. But you proceed and do experiments in computer simulations to just verify some experiments or try to prove them in a more material type of sense.

Hans-Jörg Rheinberger: I think the basic question for the history of science—if you take the history of science in the broad sense and include not only physics but the other areas of working "scientifically" as well—then, of course, you realize that the kind of paradigms that we observe in the development of physics, and in particular during the twentieth century, are not at all characteristic of most of the other areas where science is being practiced. The conundrum, or the difficulty, is that philosophers of science have always been taking physics as the paradigm of what it means to do science. This brings with it a distortion, I would say, that prohibits us from seeing the entire complexity of scientific activity, be it if you go into the depth of history or be it if you spread out in all these different areas where scientific activities are going on. And I think we need a way and also a place to kind of bring this complexity to the table, and also take it seriously.

Angela Gencarelli: I'm a literary scholar and I only have a vague idea about quantum physics, but right now I'm working on a project about the narrativity of physical texts. So, my question would point to the direction of the history of science: How are we able to construct and reconstruct scientific processes through texts?

HJR: So this is actually the question we just had on the table, asked on another level. Can you really learn about the dynamics of science by stepping from one published paper to the other? I don't think that it works—it gives you an distorted vision of how science is proceeding. So we need to take into account not only the text but also the context to play with this kind of distinction, I would say. And, in the way of how we are able, or could, or should, construct our narratives about science, historically, there is no royal path to go. I think if you try to recount a shorter episode in the history of experimental science, to describe the trajectory of an experimental system is a possible narrative. But, if you, say, follow the history of physics over 150 years, you will probably not be able to choose such an entity as the point that can give you a consistent narrative. So you have to think about narrativity if you do history of science.

WH: Just one other short hint: maybe you should read one of the most important texts in the history of philosophy. And this is the "Crisis Text" by Husserl from 1935 [*The Crisis of European Sciences and Transcendental Phenomenology*]. It's an attempt to think about the possibility of a history of science, actually, and how Husserl worked it out. From the method, not in the philosophical arguments itself, it's very interesting, and will take you far beyond the concept of a text.

Janina Wellmann: Working on the history of biology and on processes, i.e. processes in general and modern attempts to create a digital embryo in particular, I am interested in the question how one transfers the reductive methods of mathematics onto living organisms. What happens to the liveliness of the organism when you work with a computer? What is life when it gets into the computer? And can you use the same methods for particles and for the living? We study a dead brain and even when we study organisms in vivo we do not know exactly to what extent they are still alive and how to detect or quantify or define the liveness of what we experiment upon.

HDR: So maybe I'll try to paraphrase John von Neumann. He said at some point, "If you tell me what intelligence is, I will put it on the computer." I think it's the same here. So, if you would give us precise criteria of what you think life is, then that means you'll specify certain rules by which we can identify what it means to be alive. And then you can put them into the computer as rules.

JW: I want to give you an example. Usually when you have these experiments on embryos, they are kept alive. It's a very difficult process, but it's never described what exactly it means that they are alive. What are the criteria? I just had a very interesting discussion with an embryologist who is working on apoptosis, programmed cell death, who said, "When you actually study these embryos that are still alive, 99% of the cells are dead. They are in a state of apoptosis." So the question arises: What is the living part of the organism? Usually, this is the part that is never described in scientific publications for these experiments, for example. It's just taken to be something obvious, taken for granted, but it seems to be much more difficult.

Arianna Borrelli: I would like to say something that connects both to the last presentation and to a question at the core of this conference, which is the atmosphere that apparently reigns at present in quantum physics, and which makes discussion of non-mainstream approaches like that of Hans and Kristel very difficult.

Certainly the fact that the development of physics is in some sense extraordinary and is taken as a paradigm of how science works plays a role. The formalism of quantum mechanics and its standard Copenhagen interpretation are a successful paradigm not to be challenged. In the history of physics and other exact sciences one can find different examples of this kind of situation. Yet what historians often see, and what we have seen very well in the last presentation, is the importance of plurality. We just had a very beautiful example: an experiment was made with great investments, resources, conviction— and it was a dead branch, a blind alley. On the other hand, there was a simpler experiment that worked. Now, you could ask: What did some do "right" and the others "wrong?" But, actually, the important message in the example is the role of plurality: in another discipline, outside of the paradigm, different experiments were being made. And in that specific case it might just have been chance that there was plurality, but the fact remains that if you don't have plurality then you may remain with only a blind alley.

And now we come to the question: Why is plurality not there in some cases? Why is there resistance against it? Of course it is also a question of science politics, of competition for resources, but in my opinion in physics and the exact sciences there is an additional factor: mathematics. Mathematics, and more precisely symbolic mathematical formalism, is a very, very powerful medium, if I may use this term. I speak here of medium because I think in the case of mathematical formalism one may have an effect similar to what McLuhan calls "narcosis": where the medium becomes transparent, so that what it mediates appears as an immediate reality.

In this way, mathematics rules, in a sense. Through the Schrödinger equation the formula of a wave function becomes an entity. And the possibility of "mathematizing" more and more phenomena brings the idea that we have to have unification of all natural laws in a formula. I'm not saying that this vision is necessarily wrong—in the question of ontology, I don't think one can say that it's right or wrong to think of wave functions as entities or not, but it's good if there are different people thinking about different entities, or not thinking about entities at all. And, in the end, you can get more tension and therefore more progress.

But, as I said, this specific element, mathematics, which is so apparently universal, can be an obstacle to plurality. And this despite the fact that if you look at the specific cases, the illusion of universality disappears. If you look into how precisely the Schrödinger equation is formulated and employed in various areas of quantum mechanics, diversity of formalisms and techniques rules. My presentation was an attempt to contribute to raise awareness of this question.

Britta Schinzel: What I have to say was already said. I'm thrown between the observation that computation and simulation can bring you insights, for example, those observed in computational neurology, which is able to implement a kind of extrapolated *Gedankenexperiment*, which couldn't be done in reality, and on the other hand, that method might produce a lot of *Scheinbilder*, which are wrong, because it more and more dissociates itself from reality. Also the observation that nearly all science is now doubled with the prefix computational, most profoundly by physicists, with always the same method—differential equations— and whether that's not a narrowing of mathematics, MATLAB and so on. All these methods are used now without rethinking whether it's adequate and whether we also wouldn't need a broader approach.

Martin Warnke: Yes, it's a bit about what Britta just said. What I noticed in my being a student of physics, the main slogan was "Shut up and calculate," because our professors did not actually want to talk about the justification of anything they told us. It was just there and it worked, so do it and don't ruin your career in doing, say, for instance, history of science. And after these two days, I have the impression that we are almost at the point of saying, "Shut up and simulate," which is equally non-satisfactory. So, what I really wanted to know is whether there is more, say, methodological evidence and method, in a way, to come close to the certainty that we had from mathematics in the field of simulation, not to then tell all our students they should shut up, but that we all knew better what it's about with simulation, as compared with math.

Anne Dippel: First of all, I have to say, at the beginning, I hoped we would create an imaginary arena and we would discuss. I have to say, we all here behaved like rubidium—well-behaved—we've all dis- cussed and I'm very happy that we created a little thought collective. Because, at the beginning, I fantasized you could really scream at each other maybe, and have very, very different positions. I've observed screaming physicists in laboratories already several times. So I expected the worst, and I'm very, very pleased to see how respectfully you can reason and argue. So, on the one hand, there is Kristel who says, "Why don't we use simulations to really explore new sides of physics, to tinker in a way with the computer?" And then there's, on the other hand, Mira who says, "Reality kicks back, and the experiment shows something new." And then there is Stefan who says, "Mathematical arguing produces completely new knowledge," and all those three spheres, somehow, are puzzling spheres for us as humans to reason about nature. I would like to know if, for example, you could imagine that the work that is done by Kristel and Hans could be of any use, if there's any need for it, or if it could help that there is some interaction between the works at the fringes? Because, currently, you all work in your little bubbles and there is no real communication, and this is one of the few spots, here, where there is communication. But maybe it is not at all possible, or even necessary.

LM: So, Martin said when I did my presentation that we are measuring things that the theorists cannot calculate. So maybe the simulators can simulate, or can, in their simulations, find effects that we then could try to find in our experiments. I'm sure that this could be productive. But, Martin also has pointed out that we are working together with a group of theorists who try to at least model what is going on in our interferometer. But I think if you're able to simulate what is going on in our interferometers and find effects that we didn't expect, or that you wouldn't expect from our theory, I, for sure, would be happy to try to reproduce them in the experiment. Why not?

KM: So, I ask the question to you, because you asked us as theoreticians to make a theory or theoretical description of what is going on in the experiment. And, for you, it would also be wonderful if we as theoreticians find some new effect based on the theory, and then you are going to search for it. By itself, that's nice. But, what we like from experimenters is that you give us data that do not comply with the theory and do not throw it away or say, "Yeah, but this is because it's in the transient region and not yet in the stationary state," and so on. Because we love to analyze these things and then simulate.

LM: I think for this, I maybe have to pass the microphone to Mira, because, in our experiment, there were very few free parameters. And, I mean, if we don't see interference, it's usually because the machine is completely misaligned and not because something strange is going on.

KM: Maybe. Maybe.

LM: But I think that we are open… So, if I see interference that looks different from what I would expect, we, for sure, do not throw this away.

MM: So, my data are not yet collected. I am still figuring out how to debug my machine. But my colleague has stated that she does not understand them at all, and she's currently on the search for theoreticians who can try to explain them to her.

KM: But she did the experiment for somebody, so she had some expectations?

MM: Yes, yes, but her results are not matching the predictions at all. There is a collapse to a steady state that was not expected. So, no matter what she does to the atoms in the double well, it's always going to the same fixed point.

KM: But, by itself it's an interesting result.

MM: Yes, of course, but there is no explanation for it yet.

KM: But now, the next question: Can she publish it?

MM: She's working on the analysis—really trying to fit her data and really trust her data. She even phrases it this way, "I want to trust my data first." But yes, this is in development.

KM: Then the next question: If she can publish it, can she publish in *Nature* or *Science*? Because if you find an interference pattern, you can publish in *Nature*.

MM: I think she's afraid that she will not be able to publish it as it is now.

KM: I can imagine, yes.

MM: She needs an explanation or theoretical framework for it.

KM: And that was the atmosphere I was talking about. So if you find these interesting things in the meantime, you are not allowed to speak about it.

EW: I sort of want to respond to that. You have to be careful what you wish for. Experimental data that don't match our expectations are easy to find. We had people saying they had neutrinos going faster than light: "Oh, it was a loose cable." We had people saying they had cold fusion: "Oh, no, it was a bad detector." We had people saying they found gravity B waves: "Oh, no, it was dust." Experiments that find unusual and unexpected things are a dime a dozen. You have to have some argument that the data you've collected are trustworthy, and I think that means they either conform with existing theory or, if they don't conform with existing theory, there's a really, really good reason to think that what you found is stable and reproducible, and going to be found in a robust variety of different contexts, such that theoreticians should spend their time paying attention to it. You don't just find new data and then publish it in *Nature* because it doesn't conform with expectations. That would be pandemonium, right?

KM: No, but that's the first thing she should do. Is it reproducible?

EW: Yeah, but just reproducible—just in the exact same way that you produced it the first time—might not be good enough to get into *Nature* or whatever.

HDR: Sorry, I want to comment on this, because it is a little bit strange to me. I think in present situations, it's almost impossible to get money to repeat an experiment somebody else did. So if he does an experiment with his molecules, I would like to repeat it just for fun, let's say. Or to establish whether this is okay or not. It's impossible. Even if I will never get it, right? If I read a proposal saying I'm going to...

EW: The problem goes both ways. For example, now it's a widely discussed crisis in social psychology, something like 70 or 80%—I forget the number—of published results, when people try to reproduce them, they fail. But, of course, I mean...

HDR: Okay. Let's take it a step further. Let's take the experiments they do in CERN [European Organization for Nuclear Research]. They're simply impossible to repeat.

EW: Well, there's two groups.

HDR: Yeah. And, even so, I mean, I know of experiments done a long time ago trying to establish whether it was supersymmetry and things like that. And some people asked for the data in order that they could evaluate...

EW: That's a scandal. I agree with you that's a scandal.

HDR: Okay. So I'm just finishing the story for people who don't know it. The data are just gone. So the experiment was done, and the data are no longer available for re-analysis. This is what they call in science "scientific practice."

EW: No, that's a common practice. I mean, the data should always be...

FN: This sounds like art.

AB: On the Large Hadron Collider (LHC), even without the scandals, it's a fact that the two groups—this they say explicitly—when they think they see something and they start having some certainty, they make informal contacts between the two groups before they make an official announcement to be sure no one... I mean, they meet openly, so it's a question. But I want to ask another question about this fact you cannot publish in *Nature*, say, some experimental results that are not interpreted, and you say it's a good thing because you would have a flood—maybe. But, then I'm asking you, is it okay to publish some complex mathematical theory beyond the standard model? It's not a problem—I'm just wondering. I'm just saying, because you say these experiments are a dime a dozen. They are not so cheap if it's a well-funded experiment that costs a lot of money. It's not "I'll try to publish something I did in my backyard." And also, among these theories, they are speculative, there are a lot. Once, I asked some theorists, "How do you know that that published paper is not, for example, math-ematically wrong?" And the answer was, "I don't know. Nobody knows." If it's very interesting, the result, maybe somebody will compute it. So I'm just asking why there is this difference in treatment.

EW: I don't think it's that different. The same thing happens in math-ematics. People make claims of having proved things... For example, a few years ago somebody claimed to have proven that arithmetic was inconsistent. And everybody doubted this, but the proof was fairly sophisticated, so the blogs and Listservs were buzzing about it. And it took several weeks, I think, for someone to find the flaw in the proof. The LHC story... ATLAS (A Toroidal LHC Apparatus) and CMS (Compact Muon Solenoid) were two different groups that were independently looking for evidence of the Higgs. A friend of mine told me the following story—this was before the Higgs discovery was announced, and both groups were trying to get to a five-sigma level of evidence. My friend was visiting members of one of the groups when word got out that the other group had apparently reached three sigma. And the response from the first group was, "We need to turn up our sigma dial." I mean, they just very self-consciously said: "We need to just estimate the sigma a little bit more liberally because we don't want to be behind."

AD: I'll try to mimic now what one of the physicists of the ATLAS group said to me, if somebody says something like you said, like that. You know what you do? "Hahaha!" You turn around and you laugh, because when you see… That's one of my main studies—I'm studying the ATLAS and CMS groups and how they produce knowledge. The different hierarchical things that go on in there and so on and so on. The only difference is that ATLAS is much more filtered with checks and balances systems, and less hierarchically organized than CMS. That means that in order to come to a point where they say that knowledge is true, as you said right here now, it passes many more bureaucratic hurdles, and that's why it takes longer to come to a point. But it would be really, in a way, "vermessen," as we would say—I don't know how you say this in English—ridiculous to do something like what you said right now, tweak the sigma and they go from three to five and they were just cheating it up. You know what I mean? As Arianna said, "They don't do this in a backyard." It costs €6 billion, and they are very much aware that the epistemic stakes are very high. And that's why they wouldn't do this. They may joke here and there about that, and that's just the typical way of joking at CERN. I would relay this anecdote more into a narratology amongst physicists dealing with the epistemic burden they have in order to produce that knowledge, because the whole world looks at it and questions what they do.

HDR: I would like to make a comment on the context of simulation and what you said about arithmetic not being consistent or whatever. If we do a simulation, we work with inconsistent data methods all the time.

EW: Sure, but I mean there's still an open question about whether arithmetic is consistent or not, right? We want to know. It might be okay if it's inconsistent…

HDR: But if you work with a digital computer, we know it's not. We don't have to discuss it. We know it. And it's not the point.

EW: Just in response to that, nobody meant to suggest that they could just, on a flip of a switch, go from three sigma to five, but there are various places along the chain where judgments are made. So for example, right at the detectors, huge amounts of data are produced and not all of them can be stored. So people right there have to make judgment calls about whether they're going to count something as a possible event and record it or not. And how liberal you are about making that judgment or not is going to affect your sigma. So, if the word gets around that the other group has gotten ahead and the people at those stations start hitting the mouse a little bit more frequently, sigma goes up—though not from three to five, of course.

AD: First of all, humans may sit at the trigger desk and the data acquisition desks, but it's the simulations that are done in advance, in dry runs, to test it out and see what you want to see. And, yes, 99.8% of the data is getting thrown away in the simulation, which makes visible what you want to see. But, actually doing that fieldwork at CERN and seeing how those people... Maybe they migrate knowledge from A to B, and, yes, maybe people marry in CMS and ATLAS, but even married couples tell the same story. And I think that's very important: they take this as a challenge. They are scientists. They are not doing fake experiments in order to become famous. They do not even have that need to become famous because there are 3,500 people working in a collective. So, they are really trying to take those sister experiments, as Karin Knorr-Cetina named them first, in order to really come to a point, because you can't reproduce the experiment because it's so expensive. That is ethics and science. And if you question that kind of ethical stance of somebody who stands in the control room in ATLAS or at CMS, you're, in a way, saying they might be unethical in their behavior. But I can assure you that if there are two unethical people, there will be 15 ethical people behind them, and they will argue.

EW: It's not at all a claim about them being unethical. It's a claim about them having to exercise judgment; they have to, it's unavoidable. And how you exercise the judgment affects the sigma. That's all.

AD: For example, also something: before the run was starting, everybody received a note entitled, "Be aware of the 'Look Elsewhere Effect.' Take care that you do not see things that you want to see." And that's a very, very funny paper because it starts with: you might sit there in the lab and you have your second gin and you want to see something, and then you see "Be aware." It's not about not drinking gin, it's about...

EW: Why do you think they need to caution about this? Because it's a real thing.

AD: Because people want to see something new. And that's something everybody discusses here. They want to see something new. They want to find something new. Theoreticians, simulationists, experimentalists, because that's something...

EW: They're not cautioning about that because they're worried that their workers are unethical. They're cautioning about it because it's a normal, real feature of science.

AD: But that's also something where we actually differ, because you are not in the field. You are not empirically seeing how they do and practice science, and that's something I would really stress to everybody who says they do mere semiotics there, and that this is just playing with science and so on. It's not just a mere play with science that doesn't matter. There's maybe something fundamentally wrong, but it's not at all... I can't even judge this.

MW: So, may I ask Wolfgang what the horizon of any symposium about ethics now would be if you're here to listen to all of that?

WH: First of all, we have to recognize that all people coming from literary studies and humanities say, "Oh, quantum physics. Oh, quantum physics." So, the first thing is to tear down the barriers between natural science, in the way we have talked about it in these two days, and humanities. This is very important. There are academic traditions in the world, especially in the USA, where this barrier is huge. And there are some other traditions where the barriers are not so big, and we have traditions in France, for example, and in Germany. We should follow up, too, I think. This is the reason I would recommend a workshop about the ethics of simulation, because there are ethical questions in the simulations, if you grab deep enough. Ethics is the philosophical discipline that is so important, even in America now, and very lively now. I mean, in all areas, they talk about ethics, and ethics I mean in the tradition of Aristotle and in the reception of Lacan, and in the way Blumenberg dealt with it, the German philosopher. Not ethics in a pseudomoral way, just ethics as in the very strong understanding even of analytical philosophy, which has a branch in America now. They call themselves "Ethic of Design," for example. And this is very important, to talk about ethics, because of this new branding, "Design Thinking," and things like that. So we want to have another workshop in Lüneburg, "Design in Simulation," because design is very important as a concept already in this field; we didn't talk about that at all.

This is my background and the horizon for my question. After having read the Karen Barad book, we should invite her, because she and Donna Haraway and all the guys there in Santa Cruz would be very interesting to talk with because they obviously thought about that from a gender studies perspective, from a post-colonial perspective, from a complete cultural studies perspective. I mean, it would be really interesting to get them known in this field as an enrichment of our discourse. Again, with the aim to tear down the barrier between natural science and the humanities, because this is a barrier of power, actually. It's a barrier of economic power, it's a barrier of political power, it's a barrier of social power, and we have to deal with that now. I mean, seeing all the problems we have in nature, so to say, it's also an environmental discourse we're talking about. And, at least this point should be worthy enough to talk about—this tearing down the barrier.

LM: I would just like to add something to that. Because, for me, this is absolutely not about some philosophers coming and telling people how to do ethical research. It is much more about the ethical implications of our theories. This became, suddenly, very clear to me when I worked on a very different project that was far outside of physics. And I stumbled upon a discussion that Hans Reichenbach had with Bertolt Brecht when they were both in exile in America. So, they were discussing uncertainty in quantum physics—that's actually where I think you're totally right. Uncertainty is not limited to quantum physics; it's something that is there in our everyday experience. And Brecht, he was describing his situation as a refugee by saying, "I am living in a huge casino, and I have to act as a gambler who can never predict what the outcome of the bet he's placing is." And then, I read a lecture that Reichenbach gave at the same time, and in this lecture Reichenbach says, "Well, in the times of quantum physics, the physicists act as gamblers who only place a bet on the outcome of the experiment, and they choose their bet such that they are most likely to win." And then, I suddenly realized that at the same time John von Neumann was publishing his theory of game and economic behavior,

So, there was a completely new ethics derived from the uncertainty that was encountered in quantum physics, and, as well, in the everyday experience of these German exiles. So I think that's maybe what ethics, or what the relation between ethics and physics, could be.

MW: Almost an abstract for the next symposium, maybe?

HDR: So maybe I can say something about uncertainty from our perspective. I think the question is not where does it come from—the question is where does your certainty come from? Uncertainty is everywhere, and it's part of, say, the way we process our information that we get from our senses and so on. Nothing is certain. I mean, we can talk about going out, but maybe there is no door when we get there. But, of course, our brain somehow builds a picture of the environment and so on. And we live in the picture, and the picture that we create is probably reduced to the part that is most certain. Otherwise, I don't think we could survive. The whole way of thinking and processing this information is derived from the desire to survive, I think. Evolution has done this for us. I mean, I don't know how this works, but, in some way, it did it, and it also dictates how we think and reason about things. So, uncertainty itself is something we have to deal with from the start, and I think the major problem with quantum mechanics, when it was somehow created, was that physicists had been thinking always in a world in which everything was taken to be certain. And then they were faced with the situation of "we really have to get rid of this idea." And that was, of course, a big shock for them. But, once you realize that uncertainty is everywhere, I don't think it should be a shock. In that sense, I would say, everyone can understand quantum mechanics. Apart from the mathematics perhaps.

FP: What's the origin of certainty? For me, nature is noisy. Everything is noise. So, if you can be certain about something, it must be stable for some time. So you are studying stable situations, and then you learn nothing is stable in this world. That's how to think about it. It's just an approach to get to stable things, or realizing stable things. And, because there's so much noise, it depends also on your techniques, how to identify these stable situations. So there are different points for this uncertainty, of course. If it's part of the object, if it's part of your reception, if it's part of your own receivers. And this, of course, is difficult to disentangle, I think. I haven't read about it so far.

HJR: This reminds me of a very nice book, which is now almost 40 years old. The title is *La Nouvelle Alliance*. It was written by Ilya Prigogine and Isabelle Stengers. The main message of the book is that physics, for centuries, has been looking for the situations that are, more or less, in one way or the other, stable. But what physics should really be interested in is learning about how things change.

MW: So we are now absolutely into the philosophy of nature, and we, as organizers, took another resort, which was to bring up the media question, as one way to avoid this, or to put it into another perspective. Anne, I think, would like to make a short remark on that.

AD: Yeah. As you said, nature is noise. I'm, of course, stumped after thinking about Shannon's paper. And even 80 or 90 years ago, the idea of noise, or message carriers, would not even be thought possible to have allegories. And that shows how much our current media are determining the way we use our vocabulary for nature. What you said about uncertainty and certainty reminds me that that might be one of the deep gaps between humanities and social sciences on the one hand, and physics or natural sciences on the other. When I teach anthropology, I say, "The goal of studying anthropology, at the end of the day, is to have a fundamental uncertainty about things." And when physicists teach the goal today, most of them, it's to find a fundamental certainty. And what Hans-Jörg Rheinberger just mentioned would be one of the possible ways of bridging the gap from the physics side, if it could come to the point to look for the uncertainty. It would be lovely.

MW: So, phew! We are back to media cultures, and maybe even to computer simulations again. Anne and I propose to give in to our exhaustion and our puzzlement and end this symposium.

Authors

Dr. Arianna Borrelli is a physicist and a historian of science, works at TU Berlin and at MECS. She does research on the particle concept in early high energy physics. Recent publications are: A. Borelli, Aspects of the Astrolabe: 'Architectonica Ratio' in Tenth- and Eleventh-Century Europe (Stuttgart: Steiner Verlag, 2008); A. Borrelli, "Glasinstrumente und Natur-forschung bei Giovan Battista Della Porta: Ein Beispiel von „transverse regime" der Wissensproduktion in der frühen Neuzeit?," in *Zur Geschichte der Forschungstechnologien: Generalität, Interstitialität & Transfer*, ed. Klaus Hentschel (Diepholz: GNT-Verlag, 2012), 92–109; A. Borrelli, "Giovan Battista Della Porta's Neapolitan magic and his humanistic meteorology", in *Variantology 5: On Deep Time Relations of Arts, Sciences and Technologies*, ed. Siegfried Zielinski and Eckhard Fürlus (Cologne: Walther König, 2011), 103–130; A. Borrelli, "Dirac's bra-ket notation and the notion of a quantum state," in *Styles of Thinking in Science and Technology: Proceedings of the 3rd International Conference of the European Society for the History of Science*, ed. Hermann Hunger, Felicitals Seebacher, and Gerhard Holzer (Vienna: VÖAW, 2010), 361–371.

Prof. Dr. Hans De Raedt is a computational physicist at the Zernike Institute for Advanced Materials, University of Groningen, the Netherlands. Most of his work involves the simulation of physical phenomena in the time domain. His current focus is on using digital computers as a metaphor for perfected laboratory experiments to establish a bridge between objective knowledge gathered through simulation or experiment and their description in terms of mathematical theories. Recent Publications: H. De Raedt, K. Michielsen, and K. Hess, "The Digital Computer as a Metaphor for the Perfect Laboratory Experiment: Loophole-free Bell Exper-iments," *Computer Physics Communications* 209 (2016): 42–47, doi:10.1016/j.cpc.2016.08.010; H. De Raedt, M. I. Katsnelson, and K. Michielsen, "Quantum Theory As Plausible Reasoning Applied to Data Obtained by Robust Exper-iments," *Philosophical Transactions of the Royal Society of London / Series* A 374 (2016), doi: 10.1098/rsta.2015.0233.

Dr. Anne Dippel is an anthropologist and a historian, currently working at Friedrich-Schiller-University Jena and at the Cluster Image-Knowledge-Gestaltung, Humboldt-University Berlin. She has been a visiting assistant professor at MIT, and a researcher and fellow at MECS. Her current field-work focuses on the production of cosmology between practice and theory in high-energy physics, amongst other research areas. Recent publications are: A. Dippel, S. Fizek, "Ludification of Culture: The Significance of Play and

Games in Everyday Practices of the Digital Age," in *Digitalisation: Theories and Concepts for the Empirical Cultural Research*, ed. Gertraud Koch (London: Routledge, 2017); A. Dippel, L. Mairhofer, "Patterns and Traces: Pictures of Images and Collisions in the Physics Lab," in *Traces: Generating What Was There*, ed. Bettina Bock von Wülfingen (Berlin: De Gruyter, 2017), 75–88.

Prof. Dr. Wolfgang Hagen is a media scholar and works at Leuphana University Lüneburg at the Institute for Culture and Aesthetics of Digital Media and as Permanent Fellow of MECS. His research is on the history of electromagnetism and on radio. His recent publications are: W. Hagen, "Ethos, Pathos, PowerPoint: Zur Epistemologie und (Silicon-Valley-)Rhetorik digitaler Präsentationen," in *Medienkultur und Bildung: ästhetische Erziehung im Zeitalter digitaler Netzwerke*, ed. M. Hagener and V. Hediger (Frankfurt a. M.: Campus Verlag, 2015), 177–200; W. Hagen, "'Wer Bücher hört, kann auch Klänge sehen:' Bemerkungen zur Synästhesie des Hörbuchs," in *Das Hörbuch: Audioliteralität und akustische Literatur*, ed. N. Binczek and C. Epping-Jäger (Paderborn: Wilhelm Fink Verlag, 2014), 179–193; W. Hagen, "Entladene Massen: Zur Krise eines Begriffs," in *Soziale Medien – neue Massen: Medienwissenschaftliche Symposien der DFG*, ed. C. Pias, I. Baxmann, and T. Beyes (Zürich: Diaphanes), 125–134.

Dr. Lukas Mairhofer works at Vienna University, is member of the Quantum Nanophysics & Molecular Quantum Optics Group. He does experimental research on quantum phenomena of macro molecules. Recent publications are: L. Mairhofer, S. Eibenberger, J. P. Cotter, M. Romirer, A. Shayeghi, M. Arndt, "Quantum-Assisted Metrology of Neutral Vitamins in the Gas Phase," *Angewandte Chemie International Edition* 56, no. 36 (August 28, 2017): 10947–10951, doi: 10.1002/anie.201704916; J. P. Cotter, S. Eibenberger, L. Mairhofer, X. Cheng, P. Asenbaum, M. Arndt, K. Walter, S. Nimmrichter, K. Hornberger, "Coherence in the Presence of Absorption and Heating in a Molecule Interferometer," *Nature Communications* 6, 7336 (2015), doi: 10.1038/ncomms8336;P. Geyer, U. Sezer, J. Rodewald, L. Mairhofer, N. Dörre, P. Haslinger, S. Eibenberger, C. Brand and M. Arndt. "Perspectives for Quantum Interference with Biomolecules and Biomolecular Clusters," *Physica Scripta* 91 (2016), 063007–063019, doi: 10.1088/0031-8949/91/6/063007.

Mira Maiwöger is an experimental physicist at the Technial University Vienna, Atominstitut, Austria. She does research on Bose-Einstein condensates.

Prof. Dr. Kristel Michielsen works at the Institute for Advanced Simulation, Jülich Supercomputing Centre, Forschungszentrum Jülich, Germany. She is a computational physicist and does computer simulations in physics. Recent Publications are: H. De Raedt, K. Michielsen, and K. Hess, "The Digital Computer as a Metaphor for the Perfect Laboratory Experiment: Loophole-free Bell Experiments," *Computer Physics Communications* 209 (2016): 42–47, doi:10.1016/j.cpc.2016.08.010;H. De Raedt, M. I. Katsnelson, and K. Michielsen, "Quantum Theory As Plausible Reasoning Applied to Data Obtained by Robust Experiments," *Philosophical Transactions of the Royal Society of London / Series* A 374 (2016), doi: 10.1098/rsta.2015.0233.

Prof. Dr. Frank Pasemann is a theoretical physicist and worked, among others, at the Max Planck Institute for Mathematics in the Sciences, Leipzig, the Fraunhofer Institute for Autonomous Intelligent Systems, St. Augustin, and at the Institute of Cognitive Science, University of Osnabrück. His research interests focus on Cognitive Systems as Complex Adaptive Systems, Dynamics of Recurrent Neural Networks, and Evolutionary Robotics. Some recent publications are: F. Pasemann, "Neurodynamics in the Sensorimotor Loop: Representing Behavior Relevant External Situations," *Frontiers in Neurorobotics* 11, no. 5 (2017), doi: 10.3389/fnbot.2017.00005; H. Toutounji and F. Pasemann, "Autonomous Learning Needs a Second Environmental Feedback Loop," *Computational Intelligence*, ed. Kurosh Madani, António Dourado, Agostinho Rosa, Joaquim Filipe, Janusz Kacprzyk (Heidelberg: Springer, 2016), 455–472, doi: 10.1007/978-3-319-23392-5; H. Toutounji and F. Pasemann, "Behavior Control in the Sensorimotor Loop with Short-term Synaptic Dynamics Induced by Self-regulating Neurons," *Frontiers in Neurorobotics* 8, no. 19 (2014), doi: 10.3389/fnbot.2014.00019.

Prof. Dr. Hans-Jörg Rheinberger was Director of the Max Plack Institute for the history of science in Berlin. He does research on the history of Molecular Biology and on Experimental Systems. Recent publications are: H.-J. Rheinberger, An Epistemology of the Concrete: Twentieth-Century Histories of Life (Durham: Duke University Press, 2010); H.-J. Rheinberger, *On Historicizing Epistemology: An Essay* (Stanford: Stanford University Press, 2010); H.-J. Rheinberger, *Toward a History of Epistemic Things* (Stanford: Stanford University Press,1997).

Prof. Dr. Martin Warnke is a MECS Director and works at Leuphana University Lüneburg. His areas of research are the media cultures of computer simulation and digital discourse media for image science. Recent publications are: M. Warnke, "On the Spot: The Double Immersion of Virtual

Reality." in *Immersion in the Visual Arts and Media*, ed. F. Liptay (Leiden: Brill/Rodopi, 2016), 205–214; M. Warnke, *Theorien des Internet zur Einführung* (Hamburg: Junius, 2011).

www.ingramcontent.com/pod-product-compliance
Lightning Source LLC
Chambersburg PA
CBHW030333270326
41926CB00010B/1614